A Tale of Two Titties

A Tale of Two Titties

A Writer's Guide to Conquering the Most Sexist Tropes in Literary History

MEG VONDRISKA

Published by Sourcebooks
P.O. Box 4410, Naperville, Illinois 60567-4410
(630) 961-3900
sourcebooks.com

Printed and bound in the United States of America.
VP 10 9 8 7 6 5 4 3 2 1

To every male writer whose
descriptions of women made me want
to scream into the void.

My eyes are up here.

CONTENTS

INTRODUCTION   IX

PART I: TRAINING BRA

1: The Basics — **1**
The Basic Bro Code for Writing Women — *6*
Know Your Bro Code — *9*

2: Tit for Tat — **17**
The Female Pyramid — *19*
Fruit Buffet — *26*

3: Beyond the Fruit Basket — **29**

4: Anatomically Correct — **37**

5: The Do's & Don'ts — **47**

6: Body of Work — **59**

PART II: BRALETTE

7: The Muses — **73**
The Matron — *76*
The Virgin — *78*
The Whore — *80*
The Femme Fatale — *82*
The Secretary — *84*
The Librarian — *86*
The Boss — *88*
The Nagging Wife — *90*
Match Play — *96*

8: Putting Words in Her Mouth — **97**
Word Search — *104*
A Manly Mad Lib — *109*

9: Musing on Muses — **117**
Your Way with Words — *118*
Breast Exam — *124*

10: Find Your Way — **127**
Brain Break — *128*

PART III: PUSH-UP BRA

12: The Crux of the Issue   **145**

13: A Woman's Place   **153**
   Distilling a Woman   *160*

14: The Role She Plays   **169**
   Genre Detour   *182*
   The Magic Penis Mandate   *185*
   The Oracle of O   *193*

15: The Genre Jaunt   **199**
   The Final Frontier   *200*
   Final Girls   *204*
   This is the Way It's Always Been   *208*
   The Last Gasp of Relevancy   *212*
   A World of Make-Believe   *217*
   The Slut's Scream   *221*
   The Bullshit Index   *226*

16: He Said, She Said   **231**
   Breast Exam   *237*

17: The Balance of Fame and Fortune   **243**
   The Manifesto   *247*

18: The Heart of the Matter   **251**

ACKNOWLEDGMENTS   257
REFERENCES   260
ABOUT THE AUTHOR   267

INTRODUCTION

I GREW UP READING BOOKS like breathing air. I filled my shelves with *The Magic Tree House* and *The Chronicles of Narnia*, came up with a dramatic pen name, filled notebooks with pages upon pages of fantastical worlds. The older I got, the more I read. I dove into different genres, loaded up my bookshelves, devoured pages of Stephen King and Tolkien. I read my assigned schoolbooks of F. Scott Fitzgerald, John Updike, and John Steinbeck and swam in the fictional tales of male characters. All the while, I scribbled character names and plots in the margins of my own notebooks, dreaming of one day being the next big author.

I was naïve as shit, wasn't I?

Lo and behold, to be a bestselling author you have to have one thing that I don't. It's not a great imagination or a penchant for long words.

* Yeah, yeah, yeah, I know it's called "X" now. But considering Elon is still horny for neo-Nazis and enjoys his reputation as being the poster boy for misogyny, I think the least I can do is stick to my Twitter/Tweet guns as a final fuck you in a book he'll probably never read. But on the off chance he does... Fuck you, Elon. What's it like to have the comedic appeal of Styrofoam?

** "At fifty-six, David wears a hard layer of fat around his frame like a bulletproof vest. He has a strong chin and a good head of hair." Later, on the same page, his wife is described. "Maggie is thirty-six, a former preschool teacher, the pretty one boys fantasize about before they even understand what that means—a breast fixation shared by toddler and teen."

It's not the ability to craft a brand-new language out of nothing but letters or grow strange worlds out of ink and paper.

No, it's something much simpler: a penis.

Circumcised or not, a dick means a writer will get more credibility, more recognition (did you notice the names in my list above?), and more money than a woman. Again and again, cis-men are heralded as the pinnacle of writerly prestige when they can't even write about women with a modicum of respect, nuance, or heck—accuracy! Sure, there are exceptions that prove the rule, but more often than not, the great movers and shakers of the literary world craft women characters with the depth of Flat Stanley.

My Twitter account,[*] Men Write Women, began after one too many glasses of wine and a few too many encounters with objectifying descriptions. An avid reader even in my adulthood, at the time, I was reading what the masses recommended— making my way down bestseller lists and imbibing my favorite genres of fantasy and thrillers. It was Noah Hawley's *Before the Fall* description,[**] on a single page, of the male protagonist and his wife and the stark difference between them that birthed the account itself.

I'd seen the subreddit of a similar name, a crowdsourced

gathering of screenshots, but I didn't want to just share screenshots; I wanted to have conversations and build a narrative about what was actually so fucked up about writing women like they were nothing more than objects. I felt like that Pepe Silvia meme from *It's Always Sunny in Philadelphia*, trying to point out how misogyny in fiction is connected to that in film and real life. But it wasn't until July 2019 that the account began to gain traction, when my tweet about Stuart Woods's tiny vagina purse in *Desperate Measures* went viral.

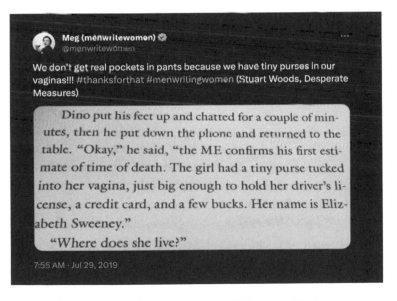

Since that tweet, the Men Write Women Twitter community has grown and evolved, and while I'm still roasting male writers with my tweets, it is also not abnormal for the whole community to partake in conversations with male aspiring writers who want to be sure they *don't* end up as a feature. But more than that, my community and I have grown, too.

The Baader–Meinhof phenomenon* is nowadays in full effect; my sixth sense is an uncanny ability to see an underlying tone of misogyny in almost every form of entertainment I consume. The real-world effects of such insidiousness are no longer as undetectable as they used to be. I find myself, at first purposefully but now intentionally, reading almost exclusively female writers, and the Men Write Women community is right there with me.

It is inarguable that the great male writers like Stephen King are talented. They have pioneered their genres, written stories that stick in your brain and crawl under your skin, and they have forever left a mark on the literary world. This makes it all the more wildly frustrating that King, Haruki Murakami, and other authors of their caliber, can't go a novel without writing a lurid description of breasts. Their female readers—and I'd argue all their readers—deserve far better.

The truth of the matter is that film and fiction are only the

* Also known as the "Frequency Illusion," it's that thing where once you notice something, you start to see it everywhere.

tip of the iceberg. The insidiousness of misogyny and objecti-fication in American culture is not to be underestimated. In a 2017 *Marie Claire* interview with Emily Ratajkowski, Thomas Williams expressed his disbelief that the supermodel knew not only the name but also the works of the Chilean writer Roberto Bolaño.* Women have been reduced, caricatured, marginal-ized, and dismissed within the pages of everything from news-paper profiles to fiction by acclaimed journalists and male authors as notable as John Updike and Ernest Hemingway—and worst of all, these depictions have been normalized to the extent that many of us hardly even notice them.

In 2019, researchers presented the findings of a machine learning model that analyzed 3.5 million books to compare how men and women are written. The books were a mix of fiction and nonfiction, published in English between 1900 and 2008. When examining how positive adjectives were used, women were overwhelmingly described with terms pertaining to their bodies (beautiful, lovely, chaste, fertile, gorgeous, sexy) while men were described with terms in relation to their behavior (just, reliable, prodigious, honorable). Surprising? No. Concerning? Yes.

Men who write women with the finesse of a coloring

* While insulting her intelligence, Williams also goes on to objectify her with the kind of flippancy that only comes from years of practice. That she can read *and* have "the most perfect breasts of her generation" is astounding to him.

* Excerpt from Clancy's *Executive Orders*: "The CBS anchor was a woman in her middle thirties, and proof positive that brains and looks were not mutually exclusive."

** Dog whistles abound as Berman uses words like "unleashed," "unhinged," "cringe-worthy," and "meltdown," and he questions whether or not Williams can still be a role-model mother or activist. For Djokovic, Berman puts blame on the line judge that the player hit for not paying attention and claims that it was obvious that he was horrified by his actions. Interesting how Djokovic is given the benefit of doubt but Williams isn't extended an iota of empathy…

toddler rarely face consequences; they aren't scolded, and they typically don't even go viral for their ignorance. Instead, when Tom Clancy writes his titular character Jack Ryan as being surprised that a woman can be both pretty and intelligent,* he gets an Amazon show. Can you imagine the same thing happening for a woman writer who described her male characters in equally reductive terms? It doesn't take long to realize that this system of rewarding men for behavior we would never find laudable in a woman extends far beyond the world of fiction. In 2018, *New York Post* reporter Marc Berman wrote that Serena Williams was a sore loser for questioning a referee call that cost her a game; two years later he wrote that male tennis star Novak Djokovic's suspension from the US Open, after he hit an official with a tennis ball, was an excessive punishment.** This doesn't even begin to cover the insane double standards propagated by political journalists against female candidates!

During election season, you can't spit without hitting a think piece dissecting what a female candidate wore and the message that it communicated. From Alexandra Ocasio-Cortez's signature red lipstick to Kamala Harris's Converse sneakers, fashion choices can make headlines before her politics. It wouldn't surprise me if I learned that staff members for these female politicians teach seminars on what to wear and how to style it; meanwhile Mitch McConnell wears the same crusty suit (which probably hasn't been steamed since he was first elected) to work every day.

More cause for worry: While the average cis woman is written with as much flair as we might extend to a piece of particle board, our trans and nonbinary friends are seldom written about at all. And when they are, they are given crude stereotypes by writers using tips out of the Misogyny Manual. If you think vagina purses are bad, you'd be appalled by what we might find on a Twitter feed for Men Write Transwomen— and while my own experience doesn't allow me to write as eloquently about transphobia as I can about sexism, I do know this has to end. Enough is enough. Cis women, trans, and non-binary folks—all of us—deserve to be written and treated with dignity and respect, and like it or not, what happens on the page can have a real impact on what happens in the real world. By taking up our pencils and writing like men, perhaps we can truly enjoy the fruits of our labor—daydreams of life as a full-time writer and publishing advances with enough numbers to make the eyes blur dance in my mind. More importantly, we can erase the narrative that men simply write better than women. It isn't true, and the world and every literary professor who poo-pooed your writing deserves to know that.

It's time for a time-out on literary bro culture—an opportunity to pump the brakes and affirm that women deserve to be written as humans, that there's more to us than "breasts like twin pleasure domes"* and one-trope-fits-all writing. While we can hope that certain male bestsellers will flip through these pages and realize that women are more than plot devices, that's probably a long shot; however, for the rest of us, this book can serve as an opportunity to acknowledge the ridiculousness and resist it.

We women need to take control of our literary destinies, and that's exactly what this workbook is for. I've spent far too many hours of my life wading through tomes filled with sexism and misogyny, which means that—like it or not—I'm a bona fide expert on the question of how men write. If we can't beat 'em, we have to join 'em. And with this handy and informative guide, I'm here to teach you how. So, grab your pen and get ready to stand shoulder to shoulder with the guys as you write

* *The Slaughter of the Gods,* Manly Wade Wellman

your way onto the bestseller list. This workbook is broken down to provide you, dear reader, a clear path to learning how to best embrace your inner male writer. There are three sections in total—Training Bra, Bralette, and Push-Up Bra—and as you level up your cup size, you'll also be leveling up in skill, preparing yourself to write your misogynist masterpiece. Of course, I have to make sure that you're living up to the low standards of the literary establishment, so each section will end with a Breast Exam—an interactive quiz to test your knowledge. Are you ready? No need to answer—I'm already channeling enough dude energy to simply assume the answer is yes.

PART I

TRAI

1

The Basics

IN ORDER TO BRO OUT with bestselling male authors and prove that women can knock them off their pedestal, one must first be equipped with a special set of skills. These aren't anything silly like a solid understanding of English literary history or the ability to write a grammatically correct sentence. That's reserved for fuddy-duddy English teachers who've been teaching out of the same tired, dog-eared novels since your grandparents were in diapers.

No, these are the kinds of skills that are only gained through years of absorbing the not-so-subtle messages of the patriarchy—most importantly, the notion that a woman's worth is measured by her appearance alone. Of course, with today's media, you've already been exposed to this way of thinking. For the basest of introductions, turn to your nearest billboard or simply turn on the TV. Using women's bodies to sell a product has been a method that dates back to—well, it's been around for a really long fucking time. We've been conditioned to see the female form as a commodity. Maybe that's why so many men feel like they have a right to it, consent or not.

Sure, it starts with the ads and the way women are marketed to,* but it seems like the gateway drug for men to take part in the all-American sport of objectification is catcalling. Nothing to remind you that your body isn't your own like a man screaming "nice tits!" at you before nine in the morning. The movies will have you believe that the only catcalling that ever happens is from construction workers, but women know you're just as likely to get catcalled by Greg in accounting as you are by a group of men driving by in their beat-up

* You'll notice *men* don't have whole shapewear collections…

pickup truck. And God forbid you yell back. Engaging with these creeps just opens the door for them; they want to know why you're so ungrateful for the compliment, why you're such a bitch—or they need to tell you that you're not even that hot, actually.

Male authors are no different. Filled with the audacity from years of never being told no, and seeing men just like them heralded as the best of the best, male authors use women just like the rest of the media, only instead of selling the latest car, they're selling you their plot. Such a talent takes time to hone, but with an education system that prioritizes men's stories over women's, male authors get a head start. Of course this vein of thinking is hammered home in every ad for beer or every mention of the sensuous curves of a sports car. It should be weird, shouldn't it? After all, we don't see grapes advertised with a cock and balls or a set of abs used to sell a six-pack of spiked seltzer.

So in order to best write a woman like a male author, you must first think of her as a commodity. You are selling her body, her intellect, her every movement as service to the plot and as fodder to the reader. The only service her body can render is in moving forward the male protagonist. The men who dominate the bestseller's list don't put themselves in women's shoes. They choose the shoes first and construct the women later. Find the purpose, then the person.

Actually *writing* a woman requires a fair bit of experience, a flair for exaggeration, and a lifetime of ingrained misogyny. I can teach you what you need to get said experience, and hell, most women have either experienced enough misogyny or have a healthy enough dollop of it internalized that, with a little sharpening, it'll have a cutting edge. But you have to learn to walk before you can run, and in this case, that means learning how to play by the rules.

Oh yes, I said rules.

It may feel, sometimes, like men are coloring outside the lines by creating science fiction–esque descriptions of women, but the reality is, even the basest description of a woman operates within the confines of a code. From the all-important tits and ass to other key features like well-turned ankles and hot, wet pussies, there are rules around how women look, walk, wear lipstick, and fuck. And while this workbook happens to revolve around fiction with a sprinkling of film, many a male writer has pulled the code from reality. It's similar to how some men take all their sexual inspiration from porn—because Brandi Big-Tits was able to put her legs behind her ears and cum in four seconds flat, so, too, can the average woman. The code serves as your origin story; not only will you learn the ways of your dick-wielding predecessors, you'll learn how to blend in and surpass them. Of course, these things take time. While I fully expect that by the end of this book, your brain will be chock-full of infor-mation, I've chosen to make things a bit more memorable (after all, this is a book, not a lecture). The first order of business is the introduction of the afore-mentioned code, formally known as (drumroll please)....

the Basic Bro Code
for Writing Women

1. Thou must recall that **Women Are Breasts**. Period. Anything additional, be it personality or a career, is just window dressing.

2. Thou must never forget thy ABCs: **Always Be Copulating**. In order for the human race to go forth and multiply, women must be sexualized at all times.

3. Thou must keep thine eyes on the prize: **A Woman's Body Is the Only Focus** for all descriptions. Thou must remember that biology does not exist; women are created in the eye of the man, and thus a gift for lascivious metaphor is all that is needed.

4. Thou must not forget that youth is beauty. Wrinkles are a woman's enemy, and the moment she turns thirty, she is thusly considered geriatric and therefore invisible to men. To put it plainly: **Aging Is Very Bad**.

5. Thou must never portray a woman as having both brains and beauty. The **Hot/Smart Paradox** is incontrovertible. Unless you attempt to pull one over your readers, the writer who forgets this is sure to toil in obscurity for the rest of his days.

Spend too much time reading washed-up women writers like Jane Austen or Zora Neale Hurston and you might get the impression that women are complex individuals, irreducible to looks alone. Wrong! In order to write like a bestselling male author, all you need to remember are a few simple rules—rules that I call the Basic Bro Code of Writing Women (see page 6). This code has been passed down by ink-stained hands from parchment to Notes app, posted on fraternity bathroom stalls and internet rabbit holes, and it must be followed at all times in order for a writer to find true success.

You think you've never heard about these rules before? Think again. Actually, it might just be easier to think back to that article you just read about that female celebrity where the [male] reporter described her tits[*] first or that ad agency that just went viral after their [male] CEO said that female employees over sixty[**] don't understand their consumers, or that [male, again, noticing a trend?] director who voiced his surprise that such a gorgeous young woman was able to beat him in the Best Film category.[***] These rules are like an invasive species, something foreign introduced to a place where it didn't belong and has become so prevalent it can never be

[*] A woman's body is the only focus

[**] Aging is very bad

[***] The hot/smart paradox

7

extinguished. So, just like how you can sometimes flirt with the bartender to get a good deal, we'll do our best to play the system and make it work for us.

If you have any doubts about your ability to follow these codes, there's an easy, foolproof strategy to fall back on: Just don't write about women at all!

Prose before hoes—you get me?

There are plenty of well-known writers where the only women in their TV shows, movies, or books are flyby mentions of a blurry-faced background character. So, with that in mind, it's time to get to work. Don't forget, though, if you're not a white guy, you'll need to work *at least* 25 percent harder...

Oh, wait...you thought you'd get to jump right into writing? Please, did Crick and Watson discover the structure of DNA overnight? No! They stole Rosalind Franklin's work first! Taking a note out of the page of white men from the last few centuries, it's time to get inspired by the work of those who came before you. After all, men have been stealing from each other for centuries, from Shakespeare's *inspiration** for *Othello* to Jack London lifting whole descriptions for *Call*

* I cannot express how loosely I'm using "inspired" here. Shakespeare's lucky he's considered a genius, because his *Othello* is almost a shot-for-shot remake of Giovanni Cinthio's *Un Capitano Moro.*

of the Wild from Egerton Young's *My Dogs in the Northland.*[*] Joining them, in short, is a rite of passage. Just like London believed, it's never plagiarism, just heavy inspiration.

On that note, crack your knuckles, break out your favorite writing instrument, and settle into your favorite chair.

Know Your Bro Code

INSTRUCTIONS: For our first exercise, fill in the corresponding box to identify which Bro Code is being invoked in the five passages. Make sure to pay attention, because while some Bro Codes may seem similar, each one offers a unique perspective into the male psyche. Answers can be found at the bottom of the page. And yes, these are real passages by real authors.

REMINDER:

1. **Women Are Breasts**
2. **Always Be Copulating**
3. **A Woman's Body Is the Only Focus**
4. **Aging Is Very Bad**
5. **Hot/Smart Paradox**

[*] London *was* called out for this, and he himself acknowledged that he'd taken passages from Young's book. According to him, however, this wasn't actually considered plagiarism because nonfiction couldn't be plagiarized—and Young's book was based on his real experience.

1. "In my kind of porno movies the girls wouldn't even have to get naked. They'd just take the guys down to the rec room and beat them repeatedly at chess..."

BRO CODE: 1 2 3 4 5

—**Ernest Cline, "Nerd Porn Auteur"**

2. "He could feel her breasts, ripe yet firm, through her overalls."

BRO CODE: 1 2 3 4 5

—**George Orwell,** *1984*

3. "...and she rode up and down and up and down, chewing her lower lip, still wearing the shirt, but now rolled up over her breast, moving like she wanted to, until she got to the orgasm part, and then she made a sound like a tiny steam whistle from a miniature paddle-wheel boat, urgently signaling a need for more firewood, Ooo, Ooo, Ooo, Ooooooo..."

BRO CODE: 1 2 3 4 5

—**John Sandford,** *Storm Prey*

4.

"Darleen Prescott's face was contorted with anger; years ago she'd been a pretty woman, with strong cheekbones and dark blue eyes that communicated a sexual challenge to any number of men, but now her face was tired and sagging, and deep lines cut across her forehead and around her mouth. She was only thirty-two but looked at least five years older; she was squeezed into tight blue jeans and wore a yellow cowgirl blouse with spangles on the shoulders."

BRO CODE: 1 2 3 4 5

—**Robert McCammon,** *Swan Song*

5.

"She said, 'I can still feel you within me, your seed, still so hot inside me, burning. I'll take it to bed with me, curl myself around the heat of your seed, and it'll be like a watch fire through the night, keeping the bad dreams away. No graveyards tonight, Slim. No, not tonight.'"

BRO CODE: 1 2 3 4 5

—**Dean Koontz,** *Twilight Eyes*

ANSWER KEY: 1. 5 / 2. 2 / 3. 1 / 4. 4 / 5. 3

How'd you do? Are you feeling inspired yet? It's important to keep yourself well-versed in the Code, as most of us will have a steeper learning curve. Even though we've been surrounded by a society where the Bro Code is just part of everyday life, there can be a significant difference in being at its mercy versus making it work for you. As products of a patriarchal system meant to keep women under the thumb of men who have been in power for far too long, it's natural to have the weirds about embracing a code that actively works to shut others out. And listen, I know that we're all supposed to girl-boss our way to shattering the glass ceiling...but why break a glass ceiling when you could just blow up the whole fucking building?

Not that long ago, I read about a fungus called *Ophiocordyceps unilateralis*, which is able to use its spores to infect ants in tropical climates. These fungi invade their ant host's body and take over their muscles, allowing the ant to act normally but really be infected until, at last, the host body dies and the fungus uses the body to send out spores to infect other ants. But the fungus isn't looking to take over the entire ant colony; in fact, the infection is only present in a few ants at a time. Instead, its purpose to keep the ant population under control to maintain balance in the ecosystem.

Now you might be asking yourself, *Why the fuck am I reading about zombie ants right now?* Simply put, it's because we share the same goal as the fungi. Much like *Ophiocordyceps unilateralis*, this book and its contents aren't meant to help you take over the world. It's a tool so that we, as the non-cis-male writers of the world, can infiltrate a system that wasn't meant for us, to slowly change the tide and maintain some checks and balances. We can't let the men know that we're trying to usurp them as we assert our presence on bestsellers lists, land the multimillion-dollar film deals, and show these fuckers that they don't have a monopoly on success.

All of this to say that the Bro Code isn't *just* a code, it's a way of life. Live it, breathe it, hell, get a goddamn tattoo of it. Just know that every time you use *their* methods, you're undermining the whole anthill and come out ahead. If you weaken the structure, the whole thing will collapse, and next thing you know women will be the ones on top (gasp). God, can you imagine? I dream of the day a man asks *me* how to write a woman versus just assuming.

But, of course, that would mean that a man would be willing to take responsibility for something. The term "weaponized incompetence" is a little on the newer end, but the experience is something as old as time. In the simplest sense of the term, weaponized incompetence is the act of pretending one doesn't know how to do something they really *do* know how to do to avoid having to do the task. When seen in heterosexual relationships, it often winds up that a man's wife or girlfriend will do a task herself rather than ask her partner because asking him winds up being a whole rigamarole. For instance, Becky asks her husband, Paul, if he can wash the dishes after dinner. The first time, he does it, but he does such an awful job that Becky has to wash them again. The next time Becky asks, he says, "Oh, I can, but you do it so much better than me!" Eventually, Becky stops asking and Paul never has to wash the dishes again.

Study after study shows that women in relationships bear the majority of the emotional and physical labor at home, often going to their nine-to-five and continuing to work when they get home because their husband can't be bothered to change their child's diaper or is so damn bad at it that it's simply easier if she does it. The same concept applies to how male writers write women.

It isn't only literary greats who write women like they're describing a vase for an estate sale, but also aspiring writers. It's an everyday occurrence that a man slides into the comments or DMs of Men Write Women with a quippy response to a tweet that *they* simply don't write women. There's always an air of pride around these types of remarks, as if it's a kind of gotcha moment that, rather than trying to understand how women ought to be written, they'll just skip around them as a whole.

I guess for these guys, the more accurate phrase is "when the going gets tough, turn around." The inability to admit that they are wrong is the bread and butter of any successful male writer, something you'll continue to learn as you move forward in the workbook. If you have to write women at all or, God forbid, as whole characters, it's best to do it according to the Code.

2

Tit for Tat

AS THE BRO CODE TEACHES us, no female character is complete without totally off-color descriptions of her breasts. Fortunately, when it comes to describing female anatomy, the human vernacular is endless. Firm! Succulent! Bulbous! Is this a description of a woman's breast or fruit? (Trick question! There is literally no difference.) The building blocks of fiction may be plot, characterization, and setting, but the building blocks for writing female characters are cherries, melons, and papayas. Do you remember the food pyramid you learned in elementary school? How the whole thing basically boiled down to a healthy diet consisting of all the above? Great, imagine that but for women.

A properly written female character will have a little bit of everything. Just like no diet is balanced if you're only eating potatoes (if only), no female character will be successful if she's only described by her hair. The only exception to this rule, of course, are breasts. Just like how eating solely pasta is a guilty pleasure, so too is describing a woman only by her breasts. Should it be done on every occasion? Nah. But when the mood is right and the moon is high? Hell yeah.

To be abundantly clear, the pyramid only applies to her physical features. As we've stressed *ad nauseum*, what's inside doesn't matter—this isn't your mom's middle school dance pep talk. To give a female character a backstory, motivation, or, God forbid, *independent thought* portends that she's an integral part of the plot. By the time you finish this workbook, the words "female protagonist" should run a shudder down your spine. To give a woman the lead narrative of any book, movie, television show, or science project implies that there was no man better suited to the job and that, we know, is simply untrue. A man can always be twice whatever a woman is.*

* That there are innumerable studies and legitimate science supporting that women are not only more likely to prioritize issues that will impact at-risk members of their community as policymakers, work harder than men to represent said communities, and are less likely to go to war is something that most men would simply not acknowledge. Probably because, unfortunately for them, this flies in the face of the Misogynist Party line that women are weak and incapable of anything but bearing children and being a homemaker.

In this vein, it's important to remember that a reader doesn't give two shits what motivates your female character or what makes her who she is, all that matters is what her body can give and how she can move the [male] hero's story along.

The Female Pyramid

Eyes

The window to the soul.
They should be forgotten.

Face

A great body is the most important thing,
but a lovely face never hurt.

Waist

Whether slender or curvy, not describing
her waist is a waste of space.

Ass

The greater the curve, the hotter the woman.
At least if she's walking away,
you've got a view.

Breasts

These make up the base of the pyramid because, of
course, they're the most important. No description
is complete without ample words about her bosom.

A Tale of Two Titties

Of course, just assembling these parts into a sentence isn't enough. You also have to know how to describe them in a way that makes for succulent eating. Writing the description of a woman's fit body should be like going to an all-you-can-eat buffet—you have options abound, and there's no such thing as being overly gluttonous. If you don't leave feeling uncomfortably sated, you simply weren't a good enough participant. But as the writer, the chef, you must learn how to take the ingredients and turn them into a mouthwatering meal. (Are you talking about food or a woman? They should never be able to tell.) Most male writers seem to think that their readers have the mental capacity of a protozoan when it comes to imagining women, and thus apply especially florid descriptions of everything from her lipstick to her toenails (unless you're Tarantino, who doesn't need words, just lingering shots of feet). Such purple prose allows the reader to envision what it's like to bed the woman or cup her breasts, and while sometimes it may feel as over the top as going back for thirds, it can be necessary to make sure the reader has got their money's worth.

It isn't unusual to read a description of a woman that lasts paragraphs, or even pages, the whole thing being vaguely reminiscent of a three-Michelin-star restaurant menu. When writing a female character, one doesn't need rose-colored glasses but rather the glasses of a pubescent boy who hasn't yet realized that women are human and not, I don't know, anime characters. Writers are encouraged to take inspiration from anything around them of a vaguely round shape when describing breasts, being sure to include ample description of her nipples, which, against all odds, can harden with a whisper. Kumquats, kiwis, and pears are all fair game when writing a female character's breasts, but really, anything consumable is up for grabs; why not describe a Southern woman's breasts as dinner rolls?

Simply put, if it can be found at your local supermarket or at a restaurant, it can be used to describe some piece of female anatomy.

Which brings us to our next section. It will challenge you to put aside your sanity and pick up a fruit basket as you select an adjective and a fruit and get to writing—drawing on inspiration like, "She was a Scandinavian dream with translucent melon breasts, so alluringly traced with veins that even as a child Tomlinson had loved maps, with their blue rivers that tracked true to the sea," (*Deep Shadows*, Randy Wayne White). If you do it right, your readers will devour your words and wonder why they're so hungry afterward. When writing, it should be a toss-up if you're adding items to your grocery list (for your wife to purchase, obviously) or finding a new and innovative term for "rump." Hannibal Lecter ought to be your inspiration when describing a woman's body—your descriptions should be so delectable that your readers wonder if you're a cannibal.

With that in mind, let's move on to our next challenge. Fruit is the most basic food group that male writers lean on when grasping for a metaphor. Maybe it's because they all happen to be sitting at the kitchen counter when creating their next novel, or maybe they took "an apple a day keeps the doctor away" too seriously and think that writing fruit into their women will prevent a medical emergency. Who the hell knows; often it feels as though these authors have no rhyme or reason, just the audacity to try and the knowledge that failure for them looks like making one of the big bestseller lists, just probably not in the top five. And between us, acknowledging the true root of fruit*—a representation of vitality, sensuality, and fertility— feels like giving most of these dopes way too much credit.

* Rhyming not intended

The ability to simply not give a fuck is something that you *must* achieve by this book's end. The only way to truly succeed is to know that you can't fail. What would you create if you knew that failure was a six-figure book deal, a TV series, a film? As women, sometimes it feels like we're set up to fail. If we show emotion, we're too soft, but if we don't, we're too hard.

Getting angry, especially at men, means risking our careers and our status, and for trans women and women of color, even their lives. Earning our place in history has been an uphill battle with men taking credit for our work and ideas and textbooks pretending that, even though we did it first, our discovery wasn't as important. Sarah Hagi was the one to coin the phrase, "God, give me the confidence of a mediocre white man." As far as this book is concerned, that phrase should become your motto.

There are innumerable experiences and horror stories that adequately demonstrate the all-too-common reality that white men can get by in life by using a little bit of their abundant privilege. Texas's Dr. Christopher Duntsch is the inspiration of many a true crime podcast, where he's known by his nickname, Dr. Death. According to Duntsch, he held an MD and a PhD from a renowned spinal surgery program. In reality, he'd operated less than a hundred times during his residency while the average resident in the same discipline does about a thousand. Duntsch's ability to essentially talk his way out of medical mishaps (like stripping a screw he placed in a patient's spine or cutting a major vessel in a patient's spinal cord) meant that his errors were never reported to the national supervisory board and he was allowed to move to new hospitals and continue to operate on new patients. During his two years at a Dallas hospital alone, he managed to maim thirty-three of his thirty-seven patients.

Though Duntsch was essentially making up surgical techniques as he operated on patients, it took *years* for staff and fellow doctors to report him.

When men fail, they fail up.

Studies have shown that, in corporate environments where men hold the power, average performance is treated differently between men and women. Mediocre men who "play the politics" with men in higher positions don't get fired but simply get moved into other roles while women, and especially women of color, have to work harder to make sure they don't get let go. And while there's some men who are willing to lend a hand, there's far too many who are willing to take advantage of a system that already works in their favor.

To disrupt this, there are women in offices across the country who have conversations about how to work within a system that works against them. It can look like banding together to reiterate a woman's idea that a man has tried to take credit for, calling out men who are constantly interrupting, or a host of other ways to act as allies for each other. While change is finally beginning to happen in workplaces, it's often at a glacial pace and met with dissent or obstacles.

For those of us who skew on the more...*impatient* side, it's time for another approach. Inserting ourselves into the equation is our surefire solution to guarantee that we are included. And in order for that to happen, we have to run with the big dogs and play by their rules. Doing so means abandoning everything you once knew. Every creep you ever met is now your inspiration. Every man at work who ever spoke over you— or whose work got chosen over yours for a flimsy reason that certainly isn't because its better—is now your muse.

Challenging a mindset you've held your whole life is by no means easy, but I'm here to help. The first way to challenge your status quo begins with a challenge. Just as you experienced with the Bro Code test, it's time to put your knowledge to work. Since women spend so much time in the kitchen, this shouldn't be a hard challenge at all, so get to it!

Fruit Buffet

INSTRUCTIONS: Choose a word from each column, then incorporate both into a brief description of a woman lolling naked across the bed beneath the exacting gaze of your novel's male hero. Extra credit if you can work more than one fruit into your scene! Know that so long as you put words on the page, you are succeeding!

EXAMPLE: *Marisa arched her banana-curve back into the sheets, making sure that her breasts, like two ambrosial lychees, were in an enviable position for Jeff's mouth.*

Heavy	Grapefruits
Drab	Apples
Jolly	Papayas
Alert	Kumquats
Luscious	Cherries
Delectable	Melons
Magnificent	Plums
Wandering	Pears

1. _____

2. _____

3. _____

4. _____

5. _____

6. _____

7. _____

8. _____

3

Beyond the Fruit Basket

A TRULY SUCCESSFUL WRITER IS one who is able to think outside the metaphorical farmer's market and discover a whole new world of waggling breasts. In a world where bestselling writers compare breasts to maps, pencils, cupcakes, and more,* it's important that the aspiring writer not limit themselves to apples and avocadoes. Language is a beautiful thing, and the best of writers are those able to manipulate it to their will, just like how men have manipulated everything from the temperature of your office to forcing women to change their last name! The ability to create entirely new combinations of words that have never existed before is the mark of a good writer, so if part of you thinks that phrase you just wrote shouldn't exist, you're on the right path.

* It is with the greatest misfortune that I must inform you that all of the former are real descriptions I've seen in real, published books. The above examples come from *Deep Shadows*, *Six Days of the Condor*, and *A Long Time Dead*; just an appetizer for the metaphors that exist in the real world.

Any writer worth their salt will tell you that inspiration can be found anywhere (and if you can't find it, you can always steal it, right Fitzgerald?). When it comes to writing women, embracing the fantastical is basically a requirement. It's important to remember that real writers view women as utterly boring (why else are they seldom mentioned in history books?), and, well, boring doesn't sell. Unless, of course, you were literally paid by the word and your word-vomit-turned-novel was, for some reason, deemed a classic and made for assigned reading.* Drawing inspiration from the world around you is a tried-and-true method of writers everywhere. Obviously if you haven't lived that experience yourself, you're more than welcome to make it up. After all, writing fiction relies on nothing but pure imagination. Never mind if the perspective comes from a culture, religion, or environment you know nothing about; a true writer knows no limits. Of course, this takes practice, but that's what I'm here for!

This is a practice that men have tried, perfected, and done over and over again. No amount of research can give man the full experience of your first period, first pregnancy scare, or first time giving birth, but they'll be damned if they don't try. I'll never forget reading a passage by James Rollins in one of his

* Sure, Charles Dickens is an important part of literary history, but does he have to take *so long* to get to the point?

Sigma Force novels where his very pregnant character, Valya, used Kegels to hold and release blood from puncture wounds she made inside herself in order to fake issues with her pregnancy. Now, there's a plethora of issues with that line of thinking, but the two that come to mind are (a) how the fuck is a very pregnant person reaching far enough down inside herself to make puncture wounds and (b) if vaginal muscles were that strong, why would we need tampons? If this were the case, one would never have to deal with the mortifying experience that is leaking through a tampon or pad—or worse yet, the terror of an unexpected period.

Rollins establishes himself as something of an expert on female biology, through what I can only assume is the University of Dictionary.com, because he accurately uses the term *Kegel*, and for something other than an orgasm, though that's where any scientific accuracy ends. If only it were the only instance of patriarchal bullshit. There's a host of writers who simply don't give a fuck—MJ Arlidge once referred to menstrual blood as a kind of "sticky sweetness"—and others rely on a methodology that can only be boiled down to "ignorance is bliss." For instance, in a sentence that I can only imagine was written to induce severe nausea, in *The Witches of Eastwick*, John Updike wrote that there was something "sadly menstrual" about spaghetti sauce. Who needs ipecac when you have that mental image?

And while this kind of bullshit is certainly disgusting, it also underlines my point. The only thing a writer needs to worry about is whether or not their editor will remove the jumble of words they call a sentence. Finding inspiration in anything from a beer can (*"She had a body like a..."*) to gravel (*"As he panted against her neck, her skin pebbled like..."*) might test the limits of the imagination, but it will also make you a better writer. That such things have a tenuous relationship with reality, at best, isn't nearly as important as the imagery it belies. By the time they're published, most male writers are experts in objectifying women—learning from fathers who refer to a waitress's breasts as *jugs* or *knockers*, so making the leap from objectifying a real woman to a fictional one is but a small step sideways. Sooner or later, a woman quickly becomes familiar with the experience of objectification, usually far sooner than should be socially acceptable. Eventually, many of us learn how to block it out, to an extent. But in order to join the ranks of cock-wielding bestselling authors, we have to learn how to weaponize that which has been used against us.

Thus far, you've only practiced tying adjectives to nouns and using groceries as a base level. That's all well and good, but to be truly successful, you must also learn to have Bob Ross levels of creativity with your writing. Your happy accidents should be turning the mundane into such artful descriptions of vaginas, waists, and breasts that the average reader will consume your words like one observes a still life. Your descriptions will be so beatific that, just for a moment, your readers will *almost* forget you're describing an illogical sex scene.

Boob-ing It by the Book

INSTRUCTIONS: To try your hand, describe a pair of breasts with inspiration pulled from the illustration below.

EXAMPLE: *Marlena stood at the podium in the heart of the library, her breasts, heavy as the tomes behind her, strained against her white button-up blouse.*

4

Anatomically Correct

WHILE RANDOM ITEMS STREWN ABOUT the room are a great starting point in defining the worth and curves of a woman, they only serve as just that, a starting point. Nobody wants to *just* read that Sarah has the body of a pencil; they want to read that Sarah's legs were as straight and smooth as pencils, firm and to be used as an instrument for [the protagonist] to create his own story. Mmm, can't you just smell the graphite? Once you have the item for inspiration, you must know how, precisely, to apply it to your female character's body. Which brings us, of course, to the very nature of a woman's body.

As most readers know, anatomy class is not a prerequisite to write a book. It's often that the only spine mentioned in a creative writing class is the spine of a book. As a result, writers have permission—one could even say they are encouraged—to take creative liberty with their body of work.* Literally. What can make better art than poetic descriptions of women that values form over function? This is where we begin our next lesson.

While it may not be scientifically possible for ovaries to jiggle (*When You Were Mine*, Michael Robotham) or remotely realistic for a woman to masturbate with a coffee table book (*The Epiphany Machine*, David Burr Gerrard), that doesn't stop men from writing those scenes. And as such, it should not stop you, aspiring writer, from jumping on the train and embracing the ludicrous. Even though the ability to simply write a big, purple dildo into a sex scene is *right there*, doesn't mean that that's an opportunity you ought to take; a coffee table book is infinitely more risqué and sexually liberating (theoretically). I, for one, would not want the paper cuts. But I'm merely a woman and my opinion does not matter, so why not take the initiative, embrace your inner

* Some of these writers, however, take perhaps *too* much creative liberty. Giles Coren, for instance, a British columnist and restaurant critic, who is still employed by *the Times*, wrote a piece where he described a vacation with his three-year-old daughter as "the most insanely romantic holiday, in some ways even the sexiest holiday" he ever had. Immediately followed by the second-most vile passage: "I hold her hand wherever we go. I want everyone to look at this beautiful creature I have all to myself. And because she is only three, they do, and are not revolted." My dude, read the room. And British authorities, might be time to make a house visit.

kink, and have your female character rub her clit against a standing lamp?*

You want your book to be memorable, and what better way to do so than to have your readers gasp in outrage at the outlandish nature of a passage? After all, since reading that passage from *The Epiphany Machine*, I've certainly never forgotten it...

With that in mind, it's time to take a leap and tread outside the lines. Our next challenge will ask you to do what men have been doing for centuries—imagine what lies beneath the cottony silhouette of a woman's sweater.

* Unfortunately, Gerrard also writes this on the same page as the coffee table incident. Ah, to have the imagination of a horny dude.

Anatomically Correct

INSTRUCTIONS: To get your creative juices flowing, use the following outline to draw and color whichever fruit, vegetable, or small animal you imagine within. Be sure to be as specific as possible. Are there wrestling squirrels? A fruit salad of oranges and cherries? You tell me! Once you have completed this exercise, describe what you have drawn in the provided space.

While the illustration might be helpful in getting your imagination working, it isn't all lollipops and gumdrops in Writer Land. In order to truly be successful, one must be able to blossom beyond the bosom and describe other valuable, womanly parts. In a time when Republicans are calling into question who has ownership of a woman's body (hint: it is her and her only), penis-bearing writers have taken the liberty to write breasts and vaginas as if they know what it's like instead of, you know, asking literally any woman.

These fictional women don't have normal discharge in their panties! No! Instead it is the sweet, ripe juices of desire after the protagonist misses their clit by a mile in some sex scene written with all the passion of a Catholic mass. (Obviously, to even get a sex scene right these men would've had to actually bring a woman to orgasm, but I digress.) Given that most men can't tell the urethra from the clit, we shouldn't expect them to be able to make a woman finish. And even *that* may be giving them too much credit. Most of these guys probably still operate under the assumption that all women magically cum when they do.

That being said, if you're feeling too limited, too constrained by the bounds of science, you can always take your story off planet.

One of my exes almost exclusively reads sci-fi, and when we were dating, I dipped my toe into the pages and gave it a try. Once I got over the miles-long expositions, it became easy to see why men love the genre so much. Not only are there spaceships and astronauts, but there are hot women whose titties don't obey the laws of gravity. In a genre dominated by men who spend their time imagining a future where hyper speed exists and blackholes are merely portals to another galaxy, of course it feels like a waste of time to think about the realistic ways a woman's body works. These guys can dream up planets with otherworldly creatures, languages that can't be understood by the human ear, and a mélange of weaponry that would make Oppenheimer jizz his pants—but the mere thought of *women* as *captains*? Not any self-respecting woman on this planet!

If you think I'm joking just look at Star Wars, which many a man have described to me as "the height of science fiction." Do you know how much I have to suspend belief to pretend that a woman can die of pregnancy complications but a man who has been burnt to a crisp can come back to life and rule the universe?*

* I have been informed that this is an oversimplification of a complex universe and storyline. However, I feel that I get a pass given how women are oversimplified in almost every sci-fi book ever.

While we're on the subject of space and suspending belief, lets talk about *Firefly*, the hodge-podge Joss Whedon show about space pirates. Whedon, you should know, is unafraid to write about women. In fact, in a 2017 article, he went so far as to tell *The Hollywood Reporter* that one of his favorite narratives to write about is "young women who have power and the burden of having that power." He proves that in *Firefly* by having the captain's, Mal's, first officer being a Black woman named Zoë. Granted, that tends to go off the rails when it comes to another one of the female leads, Inara.

Inara works as a Companion, the *Firefly* universe term for a sex worker. It is a profession that is well respected in the universe by everyone but Mal, it would seem, who often slut-shames and insults her for the profession she chose. Whedon's solution, which thankfully never fully came to fruition, was to have the space villain Reavers invade their ship while Mal is away, and Inara would inject herself with a syringe of medication that would horribly kill anyone who raped her. Mal would later return to the ship to discover all the Reavers dead, which implies a pretty horrific encounter. As Tim Minnear, the show's series writer and executive producer, explained, "At the end of the episode, he comes in after she's been horribly brutalized, gets down on his knee, and takes her hand. And he treats her like a lady."

Thankfully, this idea never made it to the screen, but you get my point. Men can think up a medicine that can wipe out rapists but not any other way to give women a modicum of respect. From the eyes of men, women get more respect in death than they can in life, so long as their death meant something.* Science fiction sidelines women as either lovestruck objects of desire or steely-eyed captains with all the warmth of a black hole determined to make a name for themselves. Nuance? Science fiction doesn't know her.

* To the men around them, of course.

That being said, there are talented women making a name for themselves in the genre—like Becky Chambers, Seanan McGuire, and N. K. Jemisin—and the world deserves to have more. While each of them is a pioneer in her own right, these authors are including strong female and nonbinary characters, all of whom are different from each other. Actively working against their male counterparts, these authors don't follow the formulaic copy-and-paste method, and they revel in rebelling. But honestly, why fight your way to the top when you can just slide your way in using writing methods that men have been embracing for centuries?

This is where you come in. Women like Chambers, McGuire, and Jemisin have been blazing a trail for centuries, but with much of their work going unrecognized,* maybe it's time for a little leg up. Or nut up, so to speak, so that we can change the game. While this book is a series of fun games and trivia, more importantly, it's a way to look behind the curtain and see who the master puppeteer is so that we can game the system.

Of course, I can't just set aspiring writers out into the wild; that would be foolish and irresponsible. In order to prepare you for your journey, you must first learn the rules of the road. Thus far, you've been introduced to the Bro Code and how to write breasts, but that's just the beginning; any teenage boy could tell you that. Now, you have to understand the formula on how to write a *good* novel. Now, ideally you take the advice of many men before you and choose to simply *not include* a single female character, but I understand that that's not always an option in today's world. So if there must be women in your world, you have to know how to write them so that nobody picks up your book and discovers you actually respect women, or, God forbid, are a *feminist*.

* And with so many of these women being told that their novel was a one-off hit versus being one success in a string of many!

The Do's & Don'ts

5

YOU'VE HEARD OF THE BECHDEL TEST*, now get ready for the Write Your Breast Rules (doesn't roll of the tongue quite as well, but there's nothing writers love more than a workshop). While in theory, anyone can just write a novel, few people can write a *good* novel. You have to have a *vision*. Some might suggest a draft or an outline, but fuck it, the best work is off the cuff. Mostly. Even writing from the cock, I mean cuff, takes balls. With so many male writers dominating everything from bestseller's lists to LinkedIn posts of must-read novels by well-known leaders, it can absolutely feel as if there's a set of unspoken rules that only some have access to.

Granted, when you think about it, that's not really surprising,

* Also called the Bechdel-Wallace Test stemming from a 1985 comic strip by Allison Bechdel called *The Rule*, measures how women speak to each other in creative works. A work passes the Bechdel Test if it can pass the following criteria: it has at least two named women in it, the women talk to each other, and the subject is something other than a man. Movies that don't pass this test include *The Northman*, *Belfast*, and *Dear Evan Hansen*, to name a few.

is it? We have yet to see a woman elected to the office of President; 2022 was the first time in history a Black woman was confirmed to the Supreme Court, and women are still fighting to have ownership over their own bodies. The fight for a seat at the table seems unending and about as sensical as the Mad Hatter's tea party. It seems like every day we're uncovering another woman from the tomes of history who was responsible for a great discovery that a man took credit for. And even in the sterile walls of a corporate nine-to-five, it still feels like every time a woman has a modicum of respect, a man swoops in to cut her down with an off-handed comment about her body, a backhanded compliment about her man-eater personality, or just an opportunity to take her idea and distill it into his own.

One of my first jobs out of college, I was one of six women on a floor of fifty people. I was working in sales for a logistics company, and while I was absolute shit at selling anything, I learned very quickly how to be an advocate for myself. After yet another man was promoted to a national manager position, I vividly remember asking my manager why there were so few women in leadership across the nation—maybe five, in total.

He looked me right in the eye and told me that it was simply because women didn't want to be leaders.

What fucking bullshit.

At the time, I was having regular conversations with my female colleagues who were struggling to be promoted, *even though they'd earned it*, because the (all male) leadership team didn't think they could hack it. The women would be told to not get too emotional on the phone with customers, but if one of the men started yelling or swearing at one of his customers, well, it's all gravy, baby. In a rather unsurprising turn of events, I wound up leaving that job not long after, when a male coworker told me I had a nice rack, and leadership's way of handling the situation was to move him two rows over.

It's too bad he didn't say I had tits as round as oranges. Maybe he could've gotten himself a book deal.

Men have learned that no matter their actions, it is rare that their punishment will go beyond a slap on the wrist. If you're a white man, the greatest consequence for whipping out your cock and masturbating in front of your colleagues is winning a Grammy. Hell, you can flee the country to avoid an arrest for statutory rape and still win an Oscar for Best Director—that was Roman Polanski in 2002. At that time, only two women had ever been *nominated* for Best Director; a woman would not win the award until 2010. As of this writing, eight women have ever been nominated—only three of whom have taken the award home and only one of whom was a woman of color. But evidently, no films were as good as a rapist's that year.

While we're on the topic of punishment, it wasn't until 2018 that the Academy Awards expelled Polanski, well after he plead guilty to statutory rape (though he was not asked to give back his award). And even then, does it really even matter? Even after his guilty plea in 1977 (no, not a spelling error), Polanski still won an Oscar, a Golden Globe, a Palme d'Or, nine César awards, a Silver Bear, three Golden Lions, and three Lifetime Achievement Awards. Three cheers for justice, y'all.

And while money can go a long way in regards to getting away with, well, anything, so does simply having a penis. When I was a senior in college, I worked closely with one of the men's sports teams as a photographer, and some of the athletes were my best friends. On a night not long after the opening day for the season, one of my friends disclosed to me that some of the freshmen boys had a bet among themselves.

They wanted to see which of them could take the virginity of any one of a few specific girls they'd heard were virgins, no matter what it took. A few of the upperclassmen lived in a house off campus and would throw big parties, and these freshmen players deemed that the perfect playground to get one of these girls to go home with them. It remains, to date, one of the most disgusting, predatory things I've ever heard. So I went to their coach. The team got a "talking to" and were roped into attending bystander training the following year. Nothing else happened.

I can say, with confidence, that almost every woman I know can recount the story of a man who got away with something he most certainly shouldn't have. It could be something as simple as all the men in a classroom getting away with cheating, because they were buddies with the male professor or as detrimental as a man getting away with rape because of his athletic prowess. I don't know about you, but I am just so goddamn tired of men getting a leg up. How do these fuckers keep not only getting away with shit but succeeding too? It isn't enough that they're given a pass, they're given a key to the whole goddamn universe too.

Enough is enough. I've studied the works of the Great Masters—read the books written by the Steinbecks and the Kings—and I think it's time they share the wealth. And, of course, since we know that men don't like sharing the keys to their success (Why else are the Freemasons—the notoriously all-male society whose members have landed on the moon, signed the Declaration of Independence, and been elected to the office of United States President *four* times—so damn secretive?), I figured I'd rip off the band-aid and do it for them. So to help you have a real shot at running with the men, I've written the quintessential guide to keeping up with, and hopefully surpassing, the men who seem to have a vice grip on the world of fiction.

To help you get started on the right foot, I've created a general set of guidelines for you to follow. Print it out, tattoo it on your arm, memorize it so it is your next lullaby; whatever it takes, commit yourself to these guidelines, and you'll be on your way to climbing the rungs to writerly stardom. And if the rules seem vaguely familiar, well, it's because they are. They're entrenched in just about everything, so why would writing be the exception?

DO describe a woman and then never mention her name. They're just figures moving through the plot.

DO use the phrase "it's just the way things were back then!" when criticized. It doesn't matter when the book was published; this is a fail-safe.

DO focus on the minutiae of a woman's body. Her perfectly painted toes? Let's read about it! Which brings me to the next point...

DON'T waste too much time on a woman's personality, unless it's her worst quality. If you can't grope it or gaze at it, we don't want it!

DON'T let women be the center of the story. That belongs only in chick-lit which, as we know, doesn't win awards.

DON'T get too realistic. Whether it's a woman's weight or how fast she orgasms, it's best not to dwell on what's plausible.

Rules to Write Your Breast

Now obviously, this is all up to your discretion, and this is only the starting point. You are the only one who can decide how many women should be in your high fantasy novel (probably one, and only as a crone or love interest). But overwhelmingly, your goal as a writer should always be to center men in your stories. Some might think women belong in the kitchen, but, as writers, we know women belong in the dedication or the footnotes.

If you are questioned on how you write women, always remember to clarify that it isn't *your* fault. It's where you grew up or what books you read as a child or that the sky was looking extra blue that day—it is never the fault of you, the writer. When in doubt, blame it on the character. They're meant to be an asshole! Or a womanizer! An off-color goon! And yes, in every single book, so of course it isn't a reflection of *you*!

Granted, whether or not it ever was actually socially acceptable to look down a woman's shirt or feel her up at a cocktail party is arguable. That men are the ones who were dictating the rules of what was and wasn't acceptable seems to escape them. Because, while I'm absolutely sure that Bob thought it was very acceptable, perhaps even encouraged, to call his secretary "sweetheart" and let her know that her dress really emphasizes her figure, she had a problem with it. As long as men have been taking advantage of a societal norm that they've established, women have been bristling against it. Surely, one would ask, if these women just told men "no" they'd knock it off, right? Alas, the minute women establish boundaries over their bodies, men start whipping out fun nicknames like bitch, cunt, nag, and a host of other creative words. Of course, men who partake in the same proclivities as women don't get called anything. After all, there's a reason there's not a male equivalent to "slut."

Men have had such success cementing these rules in part because of their positions of power and their unshakable ability to commit to misogyny. While there are those women who question the status quo, it's unfortunately those same women who are penalized the most, facing online trolls, death threats, doxing, and more from men who are nothing short of furious that a woman has the audacity to say no. For a woman to be willing to take up the mantle of dissent takes a sort of courage that not all of us have, and for those of us not ready to paint a scarlet letter on our chest but still want to create change, we can take on those insidious rules and make them work for us.

Of course, simply learning those rules aren't enough. You need to become a wolf in sheep's clothing and embrace those rules with every fiber of your being. As with all things, the best way to learn is to do.

The Do's & Dont's

INSTRUCTIONS: With this challenge, we'll ask that you prove what you've learned by adding **DO** or **DON'T** in front of each statement to see how it fits.

1. _____ build a full backstory for each female character, including what drives her, her goals, her family history

2. _____ fixate on and continuously reiterate a female character's biggest flaw—is she too brash? Bossy? Sassy? Remind your readers.

3. _____ make sure your male protagonist always has a leg up on a female character, whether it's physical strength or a deep dark secret.

4. _____ make sure that if a woman is better than her male counterpart at something, it is explained in a way that puts the woman in a bad light.

5. _____ put women in high seats of power unless it is to show how corrupt or inept they are.

6. _____ feel free to use anatomy as you will, not necessarily paying attention to science.

7. _____ adjust your story based on what is deemed socially acceptable.

ANSWERS: 1. DON'T / 2. DO / 3. DO / 4. DO / 5. DON'T / 6. DO / 7. DON'T

It goes without saying that every writer also has a set of rules that are unique to them. Ben Aaronovitch, for instance, exclusively writes large women in a way that can only be described as fatphobic and hateful.* And while the rules you make don't need to be even half as hateful, it's still important to find your voice and what makes you tick as a writer.

* In his book _Rivers of London_ he writes this gem of a line: "The voice belonged to a plump, round-faced woman of the sort that develops a good personality because the alternative is suicide." I don't care how much of an asshole your character is; this kind of writing is just plain hateful.

PROMPT: On the next page, create your own guidelines to follow. Tape them up in front of your writing station so you never forget!:

THE _____ WRITING RULES

DO _____
_____
_____

DON'T _____
_____
_____

DO _____
_____
_____

DON'T _____
_____
_____

DO _____
_____
_____

DON'T _____
_____
_____

DO _____
_____
_____

DON'T _____
_____

Body of Work

IN A TIME WHERE MUCH of womanhood is commoditized, reading about the female form as a woman is in and of itself an almost out-of-body experience. In art, men seem to adore women...until you look closer. Caravaggio's painting of Judith slaying Holofernes is a depiction of a fierce woman, Judith, saving her people by beheading a general. In what could be considered a largely feminist moment, Judith is shown cutting of Holofernes's head while leaning back, as if afraid of getting blood on her top.

The narrative is always the same. Women can be beautiful, but they are beautiful because of their body, not their power. Male authors capitalize upon this to the extent that sometimes, when reading a description of women who can gain a cup size

* *The Moving Toyshop*, Edmund Crispin

** *Compulsion*, Jonathan Kellerman

upon marriage* or the existence of breasts that are optimistic,** it feels as if you, as a woman, don't even know your own body. It becomes harder and harder to disentangle yourself from the male perception.

There can be this unsettling feeling that even a catcaller might know your body better than you did, and even as eccentric as some of the descriptions male authors give women may be, it can sometimes leave behind an unpleasant aftertaste that maybe there's something wrong with you because you don't have the experiences these well-known men are writing.

Like with everything else, this shit is everywhere too. Unhinged descriptions are so commonplace that they seem normal, so it's no wonder when we see it in everything from *Vogue* articles to comic strips. As you know by now, there's no real way to topple the patriarchy; we must simply build on the foundation they've been kind enough to provide and take over the structure itself.

It isn't nearly as hard you'd think, either. The bright side of having a surround sound misogynistic experience since toddlerhood is that there's no better expert on the patriarchy than those who have felt its impact the most. So embrace your inner adolescent boy and remember every shitty thing you've ever heard prescribed to a developing teen as we get down to the most important thing any writer can do—describing a woman by her body. To be clear, it doesn't matter if these descriptions forward your plot. What matters is that readers know the firmness of a woman's breast or the width of her waist. Whether she's a main character, a supporting character, or simply a passerby on in the pages of your novel, *every woman** is worthy of a description crude enough to make even your racist grandfather blush.

Imagining these flamboyant descriptions isn't enough, but writing them can sometimes feel at odds with everything we've learned thus far.

WWSKD?**

INSTRUCTIONS: To help grease the process, I've gone ahead and written two different descriptions for each woman on the following pages, it's your job to review options A and B to identify which best describes her. Should you find yourself struggling, simply ask yourself *WWSKD?*

* Ironic that not every woman evidently deserves to have a speaking role, but every one of them gets to have every pore described in intimate detail.

** What Would Stephen King Do?—the words any aspiring writer should live by. What other beloved author do you know of that can craft such magnificent stories and rich worlds, all the while describing breasts as gun shells or nubs or punching bags.

61

1.

Ⓐ Elaine was tall and graceful; she moved with the self-possession of a ballerina.

Ⓑ Elaine was tall and graceful; she had the lithe body of a ballerina with pert breasts and a waist you could thread through the eye of a needle.

2.

Ⓐ As Marisa climbed the stairs, her breasts heaved beneath her sweater, jiggling with every effortful step.

Ⓑ As Marisa climbed the stairs, she struggled to keep her breath even, panting with every effortful step.

3.

Ⓐ The cashier had bright eyes and full lips, which Evan was transfixed by as she spoke.

Ⓑ The cashier had fuck-me eyes and full lips, which Evan stared at as she spoke, imagining all the things those lips could do to him.

4.

Ⓐ Calliope raced across the crosswalk, already late for tennis practice, her racket bag slapping her thigh as she ran.

Ⓑ Calliope raced across the crosswalk, her tennis skirt riding up her thighs as her racket bag slapped against them, deliciously showing off her summer's-end tan and her rippling muscles.

5.

(A) Tina's face was wizened from a life of manual labor, pulled down at the jowls like there were weights attached.

(B) Tina's face was wizened and ancient. Her breasts sat on her chest like withered apples; her body was worn from a life of manual labor.

6.

(A) James was just trying to check in to his room, but the clerk had lost his reservation. He leaned forward, trying to read her name tag, but instead found his attention captured by her heavy, round breasts that strained to escape from her blouse.

(B) James was just trying to check in to his room, but the clerk had lost his reservation. He leaned forward, trying to road her name tag, so he could tell her manager just what he thought of *Laura*.

7.

(A) Monica had been teaching at the ski chalet for years now, the way her ski suit clung to her curves, as generously round and dipping as a mogul, had even the most experienced men begging for a lesson.

(B) Monica had been teaching at the ski chalet for years, and as the only female instructor, she often found herself stuck with the most lecherous of the men.

8.

Ⓐ The bartender licked her lips as she spoke to Tom. That paired with her sensuous grip on the bottle of tequila and the way her breasts winked from her low-cut top was all he needed to know that she wanted him to wait for her shift to end and take her home.

Ⓑ The bartender poured Tom a strong shot of tequila. He thought she'd maybe been flirting with him, but maybe he was just drunk.

9.

Ⓐ All eyes were on the three women standing on the corner, but only one had caught Mark's attention. The woman on the right was just his type, and he couldn't look away.

Ⓑ All eyes were on the three women standing on the corner, but only one had caught Mark's attention. The woman on the left was too tall, her breasts too high and firm. The one in the middle was too short and dumpy, her lurid red lipstick and generous curves giving her a whorish appearance. But the one on the right? She was his Goldilocks, with breasts he could hold in his hands, curves dipped enough to drink out of, and a wide-eyed innocence on her face.

10.

Ⓐ She may have been only sixteen, but he knew that she was aware of the effect she had on him. Anyone with tits and an ass like that knew what they could do to men.

Ⓑ She was only sixteen, but he wasn't a sketchy dude; he didn't give her a second look.

ANSWER BANK: 1. B / 2. A / 3. B / 4. B / 5. B / 6. A / 7. A / 8. A / 9. B / 10. A

Your Turn

INSTRUCTIONS: Now it's your turn! On the following pages, transform each passage into something worthy of a bestselling male author, and you'll be well on your way to writing your own stories.

Heather sat before the fireplace, her knees pulled up to her chest, burrowing as deeply as she could into her sweater.

_____

_____

_____

_____

_____

_____

_____

_____

_____

Tatiana lay prone on the bed, her chin resting in her hands as she turned the pages of her book.

Daniel glanced over at Samantha as she used the StairMaster, headphones clamped over her ears, in her own world.

The women walked down the sidewalk in a clump,

four abreast and dressed to the nines.

_____

_____

_____

_____

_____

_____

She was the only one behind the bar, pouring shots and

shaking cocktails like she'd been born to do it.

_____

_____

_____

_____

_____

_____

_____

He was trying to talk to the barista, but she seemed bored—more interested in fiddling with the ties of her apron than taking his order.

There were two women in the bleachers beside him, cheering their hearts out for their hockey team.

Sophia was curled up on the bed, nursing a glass of red wine.

_____

_____

_____

_____

_____

_____

He liked sitting like this, shoulder to shoulder with
Lola, listening to the fireplace crackle.

_____

_____

_____

_____

_____

_____

_____

_____

PART II

BRA

7

The Muses

MALE WRITERS ARE NOT MONSTERS—NO, even the most prize-winning and bestselling prick with a pen (or is it pen with a prick?) knows that, occasionally, a literary work can benefit from the presence of a female character who is more than a pair of boobs or a gently sloping gluteus maximus. Fortunately for our purposes, such women characters fit neatly into one of several types, and now that you've mastered the Bro Code and wet your pen in the endless font of descriptions that objectify women's bodies, it is time to meet these types.

This section will be dedicated to the wonders of typecasting—and, more specifically, to the Muses, a round-up of women who differ in many ways but share a common purpose: to inspire the male writer and advance the story of the male hero. You may not know it yet, but the Muses are sure to be your best friends, inspired by every stereotype you've ever read.

It is important—no, *critical!*—to note that the Muses, and the female characters they bring to life, should not have personality or substance. They exist solely to motivate the male hero and to move the plot forward. Thus, they should have as much depth as a teacup and should be as real as a set of veneers.

When evoking the muse of your choice, one must never incorporate the complex qualities of a person you know in real life, but instead, draw on a highly reductive amalgamation of every woman you've ever met and a hastily gathered bouquet of stereotypes. It's important to keep things superficial, lest you confuse the reader with the notion that women might be fully formed beings with desires or wishes of their own.

The Muses in this workbook are, in theory, fictional. But the reality is that each one is drawn from the stereotypes and assumptions that men make about women every day. This can range from the hum drum that if she's wearing headphones and doesn't acknowledge you, she's a bitch, and if her top is too low or skirt too high, she's a slut. Men make jokes out of it, make whole YouTube diatribes about how, on a first date, you should take a girl swimming to see what she "really" looks like.* It's the kind of insidious societal conditioning that follows us from our personal life to our professional one and is rooted in all sorts of bullshit. Is she a leader or soft-spoken? Does she wear lipstick and heels or ballet flats and bows? We are marketed to by how men see us, so coined the male gaze, and consciously or not, dress to fit the mold of that which we aspire to.

We all know someone who men would perceive to fit into the narrow definition of one of the Muses, but some would argue that it's the ability of identifying and knowing the stereotype you supposedly embody that allows you to flummox the men around you. It would seem that many men are simple creatures; their entire world is rocked when a gorgeous woman happens to also be incredibly intelligent, or when a woman is able to do something that they can't, be that climb a mountain or lift a weight. It's a superpower in its own right. And in order to wield that power, you have to be able to identify the Muses you supposedly are.

* Strangely it seems that these are almost always the same men who have a profile photo from at least five years ago.

the Matron

> "We made double time down the left-hand corridor, perhaps to make up for our unscheduled stop. Mrs. Bancroft's breasts jiggled with her steps under the thin material of the leotard, and I took morose interest in the art on the other side of the corridor."

—**Richard Morgan**, *Altered Carbon*

IS ANY NOVEL COMPLETE WITHOUT a one-dimensional rendering of a woman whose purpose is to serve? Of course not. The Matron is a woman who is dowdy, most likely with large breasts like pillows for you to lay your head upon. She probably says "dearie" more often than is necessary and is always available to give the hero advice; of other women, she most likely says something like "that one's trouble." She is often written as a woman of substantial girth, as slim women cannot be motherly (duh).

The Matron tends to be enrobed in featureless clothing that gives a nod to her nurturing side. This could mean anything from a house dress with an apron (signifying her ability to bake and be a homemaker) to loose jeans and an ill-fitting top paired with gardening gloves (to show that the matron's caring nature extends to plant life as well as people). Matrons may be widowed or married to an easily befuddled man (who is never the hero), and they often have a large brood of children who are mentioned but never seen.

These women hand out wisdom to the hero like a PEZ dispenser, usually with a large helping of a comfort food (stew, anyone?), and yet somehow they never find the hero to be the one at fault. In crime novels, the Matron can occasionally be found to say just the right thing that gives the hero a brilliant stroke of inspiration to solve the grisly murder. In fantasy or historical fiction, the Matron will be seen handing out ale and crusty bread, her large breasts heaving out of her blouse, ready at a moment's notice to envelope the hero in a loving hug.

HOW TO WRITE A MATRON:

- She regularly dispenses life advice that could've come from a fortune cookie.
- Her hobby is vaguely related to the advice she gives (e.g., gardening and growth).
- Dressed in genderless clothing.
- Very large breasts, all the better to give good hugs.

the Virgin

> "'That child ought t'have herself relations with the right type of man at the earliest opportunity. I can say that with complete conviction, both as her guardian and as a biologist,' said the old man, salting his cucumbers."

—Haruki Murakami, *Hard-Boiled Wonderland and the End of the World*

THE EPITOME OF "PRETTY BUT doesn't know it," the Virgin is perhaps best described as *nubile*. She is pure as the driven snow, a little awkward, and unerringly sexy, with features like large eyes, budding breasts (see Bro Code 1!), and puckered knees. The Virgin is usually quite quiet, with all of the personality of a communion wafer, and can be used to remind the hero of his virility or the fact that every day he's closer to his own death (and that sleeping with young women is the only way to really *carpe* that *diem*).

The Virgin's clothing is always simple, usually with frills— naively low cut (how did *that* slip out of there?) but never slutty. Her cheeks are freckled, and her lips are rosebuds; she blushes at the mere breath of innuendo and has no idea the effect that she has on the hero. Or does she?

She is typically not a memorable character (are women ever?), and rarely has anything of any importance to say. Her only worth is in her appearance and in her tender, innocent sex appeal. With the Virgin, there is an alluring feeling of forbidden fruit. See also: *Lolita*.

While the hero may know it is wrong to harbor feelings for such a pure and youthful being, it is always clear that these feelings are the fault of the Virgin. In some cases, the hero blames the inescapable temptations of the Virgin's appearance; in others, he blames women as a species for their wily ways.

HOW TO WRITE A VIRGIN:
- ✓ She wears a lot of bows and ruffles, which mimic her bow-shaped lips and innocence.
- ✓ Her air of naivete may or may not be an act, depending on who you ask.
- ✓ She's usually a student of the protagonist and exceptionally bright.

the Whore

> *"But this time when he kissed her, his astonishingly resourceful tongue managed to break through the heroic barricade that her teeth had heretofore formed. There was a clean clink of enamel against enamel, an eruption of hot saliva as his tongue made a whirlwind tour of her oral hollow. A sudden jolt shot through the peachfish, fuzz and fin, and inside her No Nukes T-shirt her nipples became as hard as nuggets of plutonium."*

—Tom Robbins, *Still Life with Woodpecker*

EMERGING FROM EITHER A DARK alley or the backdoor of a grubby bar, the Whore is a well-worked woman who has been rode hard and put away wet. In the harsh light of day, she looks older than her years. Most likely bedecked in gaudy jewelry and loud colors, she cusses like a sailor and drinks like a boxer. She is uncouth, unfiltered, and always happens to be loitering at the exact street corner where the hero will be (usually with a cigarette dangling off her lip).

She deals in hard drugs and hard-won wisdom, and at some point she will probably end up dead or dying with no one to care but the hero (who eventually realized—too late!—that behind all that makeup and sex work, she was a real person). Upon the news of her death, usually a grisly one dealt in some dimly lit alley or sticky-floored motel room, the hero realizes that the Whore was worthy of love and kindness after all, and he resolves to treat all people as people going forward. (Fat chance!)

The Whore is not someone the hero is necessarily attracted to, but rather, someone he is fascinated by. He tends to view her as below him, and while he views her as vile, he can't stay away. The role of the Whore is to deal out lessons through her presence (or lack thereof).

HOW TO WRITE A WHORE:

- ✓ Voted "Most Likely to Be a Victim in a CSI Episode."
- ✓ Has a fifty-fifty chance of imparting a life lesson or an STD.
- ✓ She probably has lipstick on her teeth, and worse, no one will tell her.
- ✓ The one bright spot of her personality? She will absolutely give you a cig or give you a compliment in a dimly it bar bathroom.

the Femme Fatale

> *"She prefers sexy. It's easier to pull off when alone, and it's always seemed to work for her—the lopsided smile, the strut in her walk as she pulls her Bottega Veneta trolley behind her down the terminal. It's a role like any other, a coat she puts on when necessary and sheds as soon as she's done, but she can see it's working: the men trying for eye contact, checking the cleavage she's made sure to reveal, allowing just enough bounce in her girls to make it memorable."*

—**James Patterson & Bill Clinton,** ***The President Is Missing***

MARKED WITH A SLASH OF red lipstick, the Femme Fatale is a bitch in the streets and a lynx in the sheets. She's usually described by feline words like *leonine, slink, and prowl* and is invariably dressed to the nines. She's the kind of woman who can run in four-inch heels, who somehow has both beauty *and* brains (a rare violation of the fifth tenet of the Bro Code), and who is single by choice.

She sleeps with more people than Zeus, and the hero will probably find himself speaking more to her breasts than to her. The Femme Fatale is impossible to entangle in a long-term relationship, but their fiery rapport will always keep the hero on his toes.

The Femme Fatale has the fashion sense of a dominatrix,

and if she isn't actually dressed in head-to-toe, body-clinging leather, she acts like she is. She's the kind of woman who has fifty different shades of red lipstick, slugs back red wine like its apple juice, and believes that all you need to know about a man can be found by unzipping his pants.

While the hero may daydream about bedding the Femme Fatale, part of him knows that she would eat him up and spit him out like the man-eater she is. As a result, while his lust for her may be sky-high, his respect for her is subterranean. The hero will ogle the way the Femme Fatale wraps her lips around a straw or straddles a motorcycle, and he certainly knows she's got tits and an ass because he never misses an opportunity to admire them.

HOW TO WRITE A FEMME FATALE:

- ✓ She absolutely has a signature shade of red lipstick and woe betide any other woman who tries to wear it.
- ✓ The only thing she has more disdain for than department store clothing is men.
- ✓ She has never once worn cotton panties, it's Agent Provocateur or bust.
- ✓ She is probably the only woman who can cartwheel in red-soled heels.

the Secretary

> "The secretary was one of those women where everything about her was extravagant—her gestures, her boobs straining against a tight blouse, her make-up, her ass in a pencil skirt."

—Terry Hayes, *I Am Pilgrim*

FOR THE HERO TOO BUSY to manage his own schedule, we have the Secretary. Typically a mousy woman who wears Mary Janes and tweed skirt-suits, the Secretary is the flirty catchall for a man too busy to date. The perfect combination of motherly care and sex appeal, she is the one who ensures our hero remembers to eat while giving a wink that she's available if afterwards he still has an appetite. While the Secretary is clearly more than capable of managing the hero's life, she's usually rather dim and is never an option for a long-term love interest.

With a desk right outside our hero's office, the Secretary sees everything—from the farce of a marriage the hero is keeping up with his nagging wife (more on her in a minute) to the bags under his eyes. It's the job of the Secretary to remind the hero that he deserves better (deserves…her). Even when he yells at her for making his coffee wrong, the Secretary takes the verbal whipping with grace; after all, he works *so* hard.

Of course, the hero isn't the only one to notice that the Secretary is hot as hell. His colleagues and friends do, too, usually taking the time to wonder how anyone gets any work done with her in the office. And then, don't forget, there is the age-old adage that while you can certainly teach anyone to type, you can't teach good looks. Even when the Secretary makes a mistake ("Oh, silly me, I didn't mean to spill on your very important papers!") her cup size more than makes up for it.

HOW TO WRITE A SECRETARY:

- ✓ She keeps the sticky notes next to the whiskey in her desk drawer.
- ✓ She is oblivious to the sexiness of the pairing of a pencil skirt and heels.
- ✓ Most likely to have the bad habit of chewing on the end of a pencil.

the Librarian

> *"I arrived and saw John at a far corner booth, a pair of boobs next to him attached to a girl. This wasn't Crystal, the tall girl with the electric blue eyes and short hair and the peasant skirts, nor was it Angie, the sexy librarian girl with the dark-rimmed glasses and ponytails and capri pants. It wasn't Nina, with the criminally short skirts and green streaks in her hair, or Nicky the Bitch."*

—David Wong, *John Dies at the End*

THIS BESPECTACLED, SLICK-BUNNED, THIN-LIPPED WOMAN doesn't truly shine until she shakes her hair free and removes her glasses. She is the hero's quiet and unruffled confidante, who teases that he's never read a book in his life while still maintaining a deep respect for his manly intellect. She reads both ancient Aramaic and Cuneiform but always needs help with navigation because she can't read maps, silly girl!

Her closet is full of neutral colors and reasonable pumps, and her signature expression is raising her eyebrows from behind her glasses. Her superpowers are invisibility and transformation: while she blends in behind the desk of the Archive of Obscure Topic Relevant to the Hero's Mission, like Clark Kent, she can remove those Coke bottle-thick lenses and transform—not into a superhero, but into a super*hot woman*. Of course, like a rom-com montage, the hero can't believe that this is what he's been missing for all these years.

The Librarian is hard-pressed to leave the sanctuary of her bookshelves, and few things genuinely enrage her more than people who don't return their library books, or, God forbid, dog-ear the pages of the books in their care. It can often feel as though the Librarian is single-handedly responsible for the hero's success (though he'd never admit it); after all, she is the one who does all the research.

The Librarian prays at the altar of the Dewey Decimal System, her brain is a vault of obscure information that she is prepared to dole out the drop of the hat, and yet somehow the only thing our hero is checking out is the Librarian's body.

HOW TO WRITE A LIBRARIAN:

✓ She has a rather obscene knowledge of rare languages, though we never know her educational background.

✓ Sure she cares for the protagonist, but not nearly as much as she cares for her books.

✓ She never wears makeup, not just because she's too busy but because she doesn't want to smudge a single page.

the Boss

> *"Time and troubles have sharpened her softer edges, and now her face is a knife, her breasts like two clenched fists under her tight blouse. She's a sexy street-fight of a woman."*

—Jonathan Trooper, *This Is Where I Leave You*

CLOTHED IN A SHEATH DRESS and click-clacking down halls in a pair of sky-high heels, nothing turns the Boss on more than telling men what to do. The hero dreams of sleeping with the Boss, but at the same time thinks she's too cold and brutalist to ever have sex with anything but a stainless-steel vibrator. The Boss is proof positive that women can break the glass ceiling, but only when they're not distracted by men or children. The only thing she is married to is her career, usually as evidenced by a divorce or her perpetual singleness.

The Boss hands out orders to her underlings like a marine general, and while she is the picture of efficiency, that doesn't stop the swaths of rumors that the only reason she became the head of the company is by sleeping her way to the top. Any skill she has in her career is undermined by the fact that she is a woman, and no amount of experience will ever dispel that. And of course, the Boss is resolutely cruel (as we all know, you can't be queen of the corporate world *and* a nice person). She insults everyone from the janitor to the CMO, and she eats personal assistants like dryers eat socks.

As a result, the hero is equal parts turned on by and terrified of her; he waffles between wanting to sleep with her and strangle her. His moment of truth will come, when his colleagues realize that he's more capable than she is and he gets her job.

HOW TO WRITE A BOSS:

- ✓ "Fuck" is arguably the most used word in her vocabulary.
- ✓ She's the first person you want to get wine bar recommendations from...and the last person you want to meet slightly drunk, after work, when her guard is down.
- ✓ It's rumored that she lives in the office; she does nothing to dissuade this.
- ✓ Say what you will, but she makes the company a shit ton of money.

the Nagging Wife

"Women will never be as successful as men because they have no wives to advise them."

—Craig Shrives, *Grammar for Grown-Ups*

"OH, HONEY DEAR!" ALWAYS READY with a quip about how the hero can't make it home for dinner or never watches the kids, the Nagging Wife is a sexless 1950s nightmare of leftover pot roast, surrounded by an aura of lemon cleaner and boozy book clubs. The hero avoids her at all costs but keeps her around for the free daycare and the jokes he can make at her expense.

The Nagging Wife's favorite hobbies are childcare, cleaning, drinking wine, and spending the hero's hard-earned money on frivolous things like diapers. The hero can never understand why she gets mad that he works so late—where does she think the money comes from? It's not his fault he's so tired from his nine-to-five that he forgets to pick the kids up from swim practice or that the last four Valentine's Day gifts have been convenience store chocolates and wilting flowers. If and when divorce arrives, the hero will always swear the fact that his kids won't talk to him is because the Nagging Wife has turned them against him—forget about the fact that he can barely remember their middle names.

The Nagging Wife's voice is as grating as the voices of the adults in *Peanuts*, and her constant need for him to do the bare minimum is what drives him to drink. The hero doesn't understand why she falls asleep promptly at 9:00 p.m. and never wears anything but a shapeless housedress, but he certainly knows that she's the reason why he is having an affair. After all, men have needs, and how is he supposed to get off with someone who yells at him to pick up his clothes and has all the sex appeal of Mrs. Doubtfire?

HOW TO WRITE A NAGGING WIFE:

✓ If her husband isn't home by 5:30 p.m. on the dot, you can bet your ass there will be a shrill call to the office.

✓ She firmly believes the greatest sin a woman can commit is being a *shudder* working mom.

✓ She knows her husband is cheating on her with the Secretary, but as long as he pays for her to get her hair done, does it really matter?

✓ The biggest secret she has is her heirloom casserole recipe.

NOW THAT YOU'VE FAMILIARIZED YOURSELF with the Muses, it's time to test your knowledge (and your memory). After all, you can't rely on this document forever! Being able to remember the Muses should be possible even in the midst of writer's block. It should be as second nature as catcalling is for men. You have to know who the Muses are and what makes them tick before you can even attempt to construct a story with them. Stepping from the viewpoint of "Who I am" to "Who men see me as" is a learning that takes time and practice, especially for those of us who've worked especially hard to separate ourselves from the male gaze. After all, men have relied on stereotyping women for decades (if not centuries) and well outside of the realm of fiction. There seems to be this idea that women are softer and in need of colloquialisms to imbue their life or career with a soft glow, and the women who choose to forego such an option are cold and cruel.

With thought leaders, politicians, and famous figures still spouting the nonsense that women are for motherhood and child-rearing exclusively, it becomes clearer every day that we aren't nearly as far away from the 1950s as we thought we were. Even with laws protecting women's rights,* there are still hosts

* Writing "women's rights" in 2024 seems laughable. The verbiage implies that it's something taken seriously, when really it's just a cruel prank made to make women think we're actually equal.

of women who are careful of when and to whom they disclose a pregnancy, professionally. Grade school teachers preaching "you can do whatever you set your mind to" feels more and more like a bullshit line as we grow older. I can be a leader in corporate, sure, but only if I speak in the right tone, make the right career moves, and not care what others think. At the end of the day, there's always going to be some asshole named Jason or Jack or John who thinks that I'm too much of a bitch.

And while terms like *man-eater* are obnoxious as hell, in my opinion, it's even more insidious that some women have adopted the terms for themselves. *Girlboss* is such a nauseating way of gendering power, made more so by the fact that there are those who are proud to pink-wash the ever-loving fuck out of capitalism. After all, we're not out here calling men *boybosses*.

How women have been convinced to willingly belittle their own work and not be taken seriously in favor of a cute phrase on a fuchsia mug just truly goes to show the power of the patriarchy. Cutesy corporate terminology like *girlboss, mompreneur,* and *SheEO* may have been initially born of some message of empowerment, but the phrase does more harm than good. *Ladyboss*-ifying every fantastic leader you meet who happens to be female implies that, sure, she's at the top of her game but only as far as other women go. Don't get me wrong. I'm all for breaking the glass ceiling; I'd just like to keep my dignity doing it.

Hand in hand with the nauseating world of corporate speak is the overwhelmingly idiotic need to drop "female" in front of every career on the face of the planet. Best *female* leaders of the century, best *female* scientist, best *female* athlete. Using gender as a qualifier for a woman's success feels awfully similar to telling her that whatever successes, awards, or merits she earned all come with the asterisk that, if she'd gone up against men, she wouldn't have won them. Not to mention the plain-as-day insult behind the necessity of gendering it in the first place. There are no *male* astronauts or doctors.

Film and fiction often choose to continue this narrative, with movies like *The Proposal*, *The Devils Wears Prada*, or *How to Lose a Guy in Ten Days* often painting women as the most base, vapid version of themselves. Men get to have depth and detail, fully baked backgrounds, and personalities while the female lead is often boiled down to Woman Who Is Single.* So it's no wonder that, on your journey to be a successful author, you, too, will need to learn how to disassemble a woman. By

* Or mean or horny or career-focused. A woman having any sort of goal for herself, be it getting laid or getting paid, boils her down to a single word that men will use to demean her at every opportunity.

the time I'm through with you, your female leads will be naught but an echo of herself.

The Muses are a starting point to such a practice. As a writer, once you are firmly on your feet, you'll be able to go confidently forth into the world and create your own Muses, but they should always be rooted in these core ones you've met today. All the writers that matter have a female archetype that, when present in their novel,* is instantly recognizable as wholly theirs. Don't believe me? Let's take a walk through the library:

If she is wickedly academically smart, European, and beautiful beyond compare, you're probably reading Dan Brown. If she's whip-smart and snarky to boot with a smile like a great white, more than likely you've found your way into the pages of a John Grisham novel. And if she's described as fat, lazy, stupid, and a bitch, why, that's Stephen King of course.

Creating your signature Muse is much like creating a brand; you want it to be straightforward and easily recognizable to other writers. In order to write that Muse that is uniquely yours, you have to learn how to recognize her. To test your ability, you'll work through a simple exercise to see how well you really know these women.

* Which, of course, as stressed, ought to be rare. Including a woman in your writing is by no means a necessary practice, unless you have female readers, in which case, you really only need her present for a heartbeat.

Match Play

INSTRUCTIONS: Below, match the Muse to her identifier. When in doubt, assume! There's no losing when you resort to stereotypes.

The Femme Fatale •	• Lip gloss
The Secretary •	• Cigarette
The Virgin •	• Kitten heels
The Matron •	• Glasses
The Nagging Wife •	• Blackberry
The Librarian •	• Lipstick
The Whore •	• Apron
The Boss •	• Diapers

Putting Words in Her Mouth

EVERYBODY KNOWS THAT THE MOST memorable characters are the one with a catchphrase. I mean, why else do you think there's a gazillion comic books and superhero movies? It's certainly not for the plot! A one-liner can make up for a lot—bad writing, plot holes, an ending that simply doesn't make sense. I don't know about you, but few things bring me as much as joy as predicting the female character's next line that will forgive our male lead of doing something wildly off base. In James Wisher's *Darkness Rising*, Jen forgives her brother, Damien, for ogling her breasts because "they make an excellent distraction when I fight men."

One-liners said by female characters aren't necessarily meant to be zingers or even particularly memorable. Instead, they're the soothing rationale to compensate for a man's actions. Sometimes it's the blasé everyday occurrence of eyeing a great set of tits. Other times it's Paula saying, "If one loves a man, one naturally expects him to assert himself at times, otherwise how can one possibly respect him?"—a one-liner necessary to convince the reader that yes, she does get turned on by being beaten and raped.*

Dialogue is an unavoidable tool for conveying your character's thoughts and feelings, so it's key that you learn how to speak for the Muses, since women can't speak for themselves. After all, they are still women, and we all know that that isn't enough to keep people reading. And now that you've successfully paired each Muse to her most base association, you're ready to move on to the next step. To be clear, this section only works on the odd chance your Muse actually speaks in your novel,** in which case, you'll need to know what they ought to say. This section will quiz you on the pieces of dialogue each Muse is most likely to say and challenge you to create your own female one-liner (that serves the protagonist, of course).

* This not-at-all-problematic piece of dialogue is in *The Black Baroness*, after Dennis Wheatley writes, "She was a strong, highly-sexed young woman who would thoroughly enjoy occasional rows with her lovers and derive tremendous kick from a mild-beating up in which she was finally possessed forcibly, so that her sobs of anger gave way almost imperceptibly to gasps of passionate emotion."

** Which, honestly, think about carefully. Remember—how does it help *men*? When was the last time a man wanted to see a woman open her mouth for anything but a career-forwarding or congratulatory blow job?

It's no surprise, really, given that men have been making fun of the way women speak for ages, and it doesn't look like it's stopping anytime soon. A Valley Girl accent, vocal fry, and language modifiers like "like" are ripe for mockery, masterfully turned, somehow, into a signifier that the woman speaking is an idiot who can only string two words together if they're about shopping. Why "bro" and the indistinguishable grunts of men at sports bars isn't fodder for a similar joke is beyond my pay grade. I'm just a woman, after all.[*]

* But the answer is the patriarchy. Make fun of a woman and bring a room to their knees with laughter with your comedy special. Make fun of a man and get called an unfunny bitch and maybe get followed home.

Let's Get Vocal

INSTRUCTIONS: Meet Joel, he is our Protagonist for this exercise. On the following pages fill in the bubbles with how each Muse would respond to Joel's situation.

EXAMPLE: Standing in the middle of the laundromat, folding his socks, was not where Percy had expected to meet the love of his life. Considering she was balling up a red-hot G-string to throw into the wash, maybe she was better suited for a quick romp in his freshly washed sheets. Watching her parcel out the perfect ratio of fabric softener to laundry detergent was intoxicating, her every movement leading him to picture the way each article of clothing hung on her body.

The harsh buzz of the dryer was a jolt to his system, just the one he needed to inspire him to say something to her. The dichotomy of her handling her bright-colored panties and pulling out virgin white sheets was enough to make his dick twitch. Setting down his folded trousers with an air of finality, he was about to walk toward her when she spoke, not even looking up.

> Don't bother. I haven't had coffee yet and I've got a hangover from hell, so please hear me when I say I am SO not in the mood to tell some average-looking tech bro that I'd rather eat a Louboutin than talk to him.

THE BOSS

Joel had been gone at work all day, and everything hurt. His eyes, his brain, his *body*. When you were someone of his stature, sitting in a car all day with your knees up to your chin was no small feat. He could feel the pain, in his back, his neck, with every step up the garden path. As he limped toward his front door, from the corner of his eye he could see his elderly neighbor Dora in her garden, elbow-deep in carrots and parsnips. He extended a hand in a wave, wincing just a bit. Dora noticed and rose to her knees, wiping the dirt and muck on her patched trousers.

THE MATRON

He'd been a professor for a long time, and by now was bored of the rote students that filtered in through the door. They were all the same, with their base ideas of what *Jonathan Livingston Seagull* was about; it was like teaching kindergarteners advanced philosophy. But Connie was different. She seemed to get it, to really get it, the introspective musings and the deep meanings. Now as she sat across from him during his office hours, was an opportunity for him to test her, see if she had the meddle he thought she did. Joel put his feet up on the desk and stretched his arms out behind him, "Have you ever thought about it, Connie?" He asked. "Taking flight and doing anything you want because *you* want it? What would you do if there were no consequences?" Connie leaned forward, resting her elbows on the table and her chin in her hands. Joel could just see the sunburned tops of her breasts, like blood oranges in the sun. She licked her lips and then spoke,

THE VIRGIN

It was just the two of them, not against the world but against each other. This wasn't sparring; it was a match to the death—Joel with a pistol and Ramona with her pair of knives. As they danced around each other, he didn't know what he wanted to do more, murder her or fuck her. She didn't make it easy, you know. She was dressed in some sort of skin-tight tactical gear and tall boots with a practical heel. Everything about her was deadly, from the glint off the dagger to the steep curve of her waist. Even her hair, bluntly cut short so as not to get in the way of any dangerous maneuvers. "I could do this all night," said Joel, meaning every word of it. Still, he couldn't be too safe, he raised the pistol, centering it on her breast. Before he could blink, she'd ducked his arm,

THE FEMME FATALE

You need to be able to identify a Muse in less time than it takes James Bond to undress an icy blond with his eyes. If men can claim that they can spot a slut across the bar, you'll need to be able to do it, too, but faster. Spotting a Muse with the speed of a man insulting a woman who doesn't want him doesn't happen overnight, but with a little help you'll be an expert before you know it.

Word Search

INSTRUCTIONS: To help you do just that, I've made a handy word search. Sure, it's not quite the same as spotting a real woman, but real women have no substance, anyways, so really, what's the difference? If you can find every Muse, you'll be well on your way to being a member of the canon of bestselling fiction writers.

TIP: Appropriately, this quiz is paired best with a martini—shaken, not stirred.

BONUS: Solve this question by finding the answer in the word search. If you think a woman is great, she's _____.

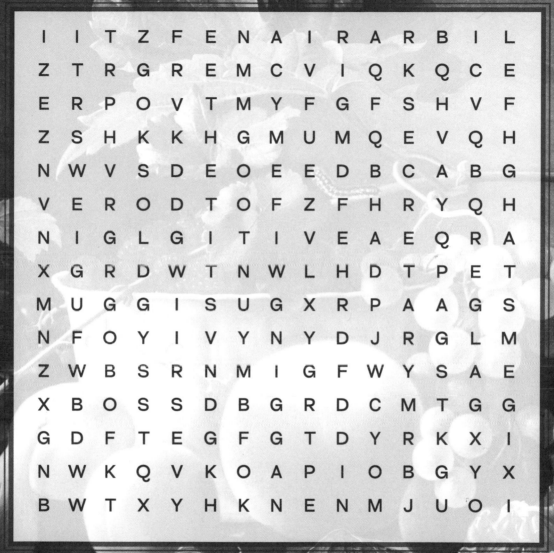

```
I  I  T  Z  F  E  N  A  I  R  A  R  B  I  L
Z  T  R  G  R  E  M  C  V  I  Q  K  Q  C  E
E  R  P  O  V  T  M  Y  F  G  F  S  H  V  F
Z  S  H  K  K  M  H  G  M  U  M  Q  E  V  H
N  W  V  S  D  E  O  E  E  D  B  C  A  B  G
V  E  R  O  D  T  O  F  Z  F  H  R  Y  Q  H
N  I  G  L  G  I  T  I  V  E  A  E  Q  R  A
X  G  R  D  W  T  N  W  L  H  D  T  P  E  T
M  U  G  G  I  S  U  G  X  R  P  A  A  G  S
N  F  O  Y  I  V  Y  N  Y  D  J  R  G  L  M
Z  W  B  S  R  N  M  I  G  F  W  Y  S  A  E
X  B  O  S  S  D  B  G  R  D  C  M  T  G  G
G  D  F  T  E  G  F  G  T  D  Y  R  K  X  I
N  W  K  Q  V  K  O  A  P  I  O  B  G  Y  X
B  W  T  X  Y  H  K  N  E  N  M  J  U  O  I
```

BONUS: THE TITS

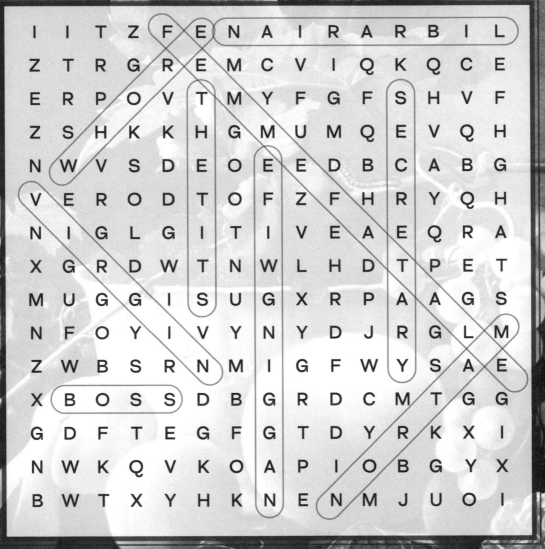

As the Muses have taught us, it's important to establish a woman's profession—whether the world's oldest or something more new-fangled like teacher, manicurist, or senator.[*] But how you select and describe that profession is a challenge that must be approached with a healthy dollop of misogyny. After all, the prospect of a woman working outside the home is still a dicey proposition. With all this in mind, let us learn from the best and examine this text from J. G. Ballard, whose novels have been turned into films starring Christian Bale as well as short-listed for awards like the Booker Prize. He has also earned a place in the *Collins English Dictionary* as his last name has become a recognized adjective—Ballardian. Now that's what we call big dick energy!

In the following entry, from his 1996 novel *Cocaine Nights*, Ballard walks the reader through a drive-by encounter with "a Spanish woman." Notice how he makes instantaneous assumptions about the woman, based only on her appearance. Rather than simply describe what she looks like, Ballard turns every line into sexual innuendo. And that's where the magic happens.

[*] A warning: Giving a female character a position of leadership like being a senator or congresswoman opens up a whole can of words. First, it implies women can lead. Then, that enough people *think* a woman can lead that they'd actually vote her into office. We recommend never having a woman in a position of true political power unless you've built a political system where her role is just for show, anyways.

sets the sexual stage

Irritated by the delay, I was tempted to drive around the

not beautiful

van. Behind me, a handsome Spanish woman sat at the

imagining her topless

wheel of an open-topped Mercedes, remaking her lipstick

again, not pretty

over a strong mouth designed for any activity other

doesn't have to try

like FELLATIO!!

than eating. Intrigued by her lazy sexual confidence, I

next time it'll be a dick

innuendo

smiled as she fingered her mascara and lightly brushed

yes, she's lazy

the undersides of her eyelashes like an indolent lover.

the only jobs for hot women

Who was she—a nightclub cashier, a property tycoon's

not wife...

mistress, or a local prostitute returning to La Linea with

DO YOU GET IT? SHE HAS SEX!!

a fresh stock of condoms and sex aids?

By using a similar formula as Ballard, and other literary titans, aspiring bestselling writers like you can follow in their *New York Times* footsteps. Now, I know that writing a whole passage can be intimidating, so for now, take a stab at adding your own twist to some paragraphs that men have already written. Feel free to add your own editorial color. Whatever you create will be better than whatever they got published.

A Manly Mad Lib

INSTRUCTIONS: Fill in the blanks on the following pages as a bestselling male writer would:

Irritated by the delay, I was _____ to drive around
(SEXUAL VERB)

the van. Behind me, a/an _____ _____
(ADJECTIVE) (NATIONALITY)

woman sat at the wheel of a/an _____, remaking
(TYPE OF CAR)

her _____ over a/an _____ _____
(TYPE OF MAKEUP) (ADJECTIVE) (FACIAL

_____ designed for _____. Intrigued by
FEATURE) (SEXUAL INNUENDO)

her _____ sexual confidence, I smiled as she _____
(ADJECTIVE) (SEXUAL

_____ her mascara and lightly brushed the undersides
VERB)

of her_____ like a/an _____ lover.
(FACIAL FEATURE) (ADJECTIVE)

Who was she—a _____, a _____, or a local
(JOB) (JOB)

_____ returning to La Linea with a fresh stock
(JOB)

of _____?
(JOB-RELATED ITEM)

J. G. Ballard's *Cocaine Nights*

If only his _____ buddies
(COLLEGE CLASS)

could see him now, sitting across from

this _____. The only negative
(SEXUAL NOUN)

was the nasty rumor. Surely she couldn't go

for women. She was too _____, too
(ADJECTIVE)

_____, too _____
(DIFFERENT ADJECTIVE)   (YES, YET ANOTHER

_____ to the opposite sex. She was
ADJECTIVE)

destined to be a _____!
(FEMALE CAREER)

John Grisham's *King of Torts*

A MANLY MAD LIB

Often some stray association she could not even

name sent a _____ throb through
                (VERB)

her _____ and _____
        (BODY PART)   (BODY

_____. Arthur and she seemed stuck in the
PART)

_____ of _____. The strong
    (LOCATION)   (NOUN)

_____ that grew from Arthur
        (PLANT PART)

was like some secret self. Real life commenced

here. This was the _____ _____
                        (ADJECTIVE)   (ROOM

_____ of being, the dark _____
IN HOUSE)   (ADJECTIVE)

_____ rooms.
        (NOUN)

Scott Turow's *Reversible Errors*

A MANLY MAD LIB

I looked at my girlfriend, perched on the edge of

the bed. She was _____. And she liked
                    (ADJECTIVE)

_____ and
(NOUN, SOMETHING ONLY MEN LIKE)

_____
(PROPER   NOUN,   SOMETHING   ONLY   MEN   LIKE)

_____. She played
(FORM OF ENTERTAINMENT)

_____ with me—and was good at
(SPORT/GAME)

it. We watched _____ together.
                   (SPORT/GAME)

She was a _____ fan, but that was
                (SPORTS TEAM)

one of her only flaws.

James Patterson & Michael Ledwidge's *Zoo*

Then I think of the _____ sensation of Asunción's
(VERB)

body. I notice the contrast between her _____, _____,
(ADJECTIVE)   (COLOR)

_____, _____ hair and the _____ of her
(ADJECTIVE)   (ADJECTIVE)   (FACIAL EXPRESSION)

_____, the wild _____ of her short hair,
(FEMALE ANATOMY)   (NOUN)

_____ like a _____, indomitable like a _____,
(MOVEMENT)   (ANIMAL)   (ANIMAL)

that forces me to _____, to_____ her
(VERB)   (VERB, SEXUAL INNUENDO)

if only to save myself from her, to lose myself in her in order to

conceal with my own _____ hair the wild _____
(BODY PART)   (PLACE IN

_____ that grows _____ Asunción's _____,
NATURE)   (PREPOSITION)   (BODY PART)

ascending through the _____ of Venus and then climbing
(NOUN)

the _____ along the womb, longing to _____ the
(PLANT)   (VERB)

_____, that fountain of life...
(BODY PART)

Carlos Fuentes's *Vlad*

The woman had a good set of

_____ on her, there
(BODY PART)

would be a fine _____ down
(NOUN)

there between them. She

could have just about as many

_____ as she wanted.
(PLURAL NOUN)

Stephen King's *The Stand*

A
MANLY
MAD LIB

9

Musing on Muses

THE SKILLS YOU'VE BUILT FROM inserting yourself into a man's writings will now help you come to the (ahem) climax of this section. A benefit of this knowledge is that, as long as you continue to practice, you'll also be adequately prepared to catcall a hot broad or hit on a scantily clad woman under the flashing lights of a pounding nightclub. You're also now ready to actually *write.** The practice sections and fill-in-the-blanks have filled your head with the Way of Male Writers, which means it is now time for you to pick up a pen and take to the paper. Remember that fear is feminine; men don't fail, they simply listen and learn, take a step back, or reevaluate.

* Though the truly successful writers are simply good at marketing and hiring fantastic ghostwriters,, we believe in teaching the ancient art of writing. *Then* you can hire an army of ghostwriters.

Your Way with Words

PROMPT: Taking inspiration from the men who came before you and the worst novels you've ever read, use the following pages to write a scene featuring one of the Muses you've just met, in the style of the male writer of your choice. Maybe that means writing a horror scene featuring the Virgin or a political thriller with the Librarian solving an integral part of the puzzle; whatever it is, transport yourself into the imagined shoes of a male writer and behold the art you produce!

This is an excellent opportunity to practically apply what you were practicing above, so don't hesitate to experiment with adjectives, sample sexualizing a different part of anatomy, or turn a verb into a never-before-heard sexual innuendo. We'll give you plenty of space, so there's no need to be concise. After all, some of the most renowned writers are also blustering airbags.

Don't be mistaken, this does not mean simply flying off the handle and creating in the old ways. To be successful, you must make sure you use the tools you've been taught. Use fruits as breasts, the catchwords as inspiration and the tropes as truth. The more ridiculous it sounds in your head, the better it will sell to the masses!

A Tale of Two Titties

A Tale of Two Titties

IF YOU'VE MADE IT THIS far—great job! But it's not over yet... Before being published, every male author must master a set of skills unlike any other. Of course, male writers don't have to take a test; a byproduct of the patriarchy is that most men have been marinating in its bullshit since birth. Phrases like "boys will be boys" are essentially an American motto at this point, and having reaped the reward of a patriarchal society for so long, most men are happy to remain mired in it. Breaking free of it means equal footing with others, which, in turn, means that the ability to dominate due to a protean boost is no longer on the table.[*]

Those of us who weren't raised as men know the effects of the patriarchy just as well, if not better, than most men. However, there's a difference between being able to recognize misogyny and actively weaponizing it so as to benefit from it. Hopefully, this test will serve as a barometer to identify how much you've learned and if you're ready to take the patriarchy by the balls and wield it for yourself.

See if you're on track to world domination and fame by testing the knowledge you've learned thus far with the quiz on the next page. If you don't pass, it's back to the beginning.

[*] While I have no idea if males have dominated since humans walked out of the bacterial bathwaters of the ocean, I do know that history has been written and rewritten to put men on top. It would still be annoying, though perhaps less so, if this Men Are Best mindset began and ended at humanity, but alas, it doesn't. Male lions get the credit for being kings of the pride when, really, it's lionesses, and it's due to sex bias that scientists favor experimenting on male cells and animals, skewing results to show how something impacts men over women.

BREAST EXAM

1. **When describing a female character, you should always prioritize her appearance.**

   Ⓐ True
   Ⓑ False

2. **Which of the following is an appropriate job for a female character?**

   Ⓐ Nurse
   Ⓑ Doctor
   Ⓒ Engineer

3. **Which one of the following is not a Muse?**

   Ⓐ Femme Fatale
   Ⓑ Secretary
   Ⓒ Superhero
   Ⓓ Boss

4. **Which of the following could be seen as fatal flaws for female characters? (Circle all that apply.)**

   Ⓐ Chooses to order takeout instead of cooking you dinner
   Ⓑ Likes men *and* women
   Ⓒ Drinks beer like one of the guys
   Ⓓ Needs you to tell her how pretty she is

5. **Should writer's block occur with a female character, a simple fix is to:**

   Ⓐ Build out the character to ensure they have range
   Ⓑ Ensure the book passes the Bechdel Test
   Ⓒ Insert a sex scene

6. **Which Muse is most likely to be caught in public with rollers in her hair?**

Ⓐ The Virgin

Ⓑ The Nagging Wife

Ⓒ The Matron

Ⓓ The Librarian

7. **If your male character is hitting on a woman who says she's a lesbian, he should reply with:**

Ⓐ "You just haven't been with the right man."

Ⓑ "I'm sorry for overstepping; have a good night."

Ⓒ "My mistake, will you accept this drink as an apology?"

8. **When struggling to describe a female character, you should add:**

Ⓐ A generic facial feature

Ⓑ Information about her career

Ⓒ Dialogue for her to express herself

Ⓓ A sexual adjective

9. **What goal should giving a female character a one-liner accomplish?**

Ⓐ Making her memorable

Ⓑ Calling attention to the male protagonist

Ⓒ Identify her as the main character

10. **When writing a description of a part of anatomy you should rely on:**

Ⓐ The obscene, to stay in the reader's mind

Ⓑ The realistic, in order to stay true to real life

Ⓒ The scientific, to maintain the utmost accuracy

ANSWER BANK: 1. A / 2. A / 3. C / 4. A, B & C / 5. C / 6. B / 7. A / 8. D / 9. B / 10. A

Find Your Way

10

IT'S IMPORTANT FOR ANY WRITER who aspires to join the greats to be able to write themselves out of a wet paper bag. Writer's block is an unbiased foe who will eventually prey on even the luckiest of us, and while the Muses are valuable tools, they can't solve everything! But fear not, dear reader. Admitting to writer's block is for babies, so you can feel free to blame the Muses—and other women—for the faltering.

As any successful writer will tell you, sometimes the best way out of writer's block is to shake things up. We're no Thoreau; there's no reason to lock ourselves up in a tiny cabin and wait for inspiration to strike—we make our own luck!

In this section, we'll help you find your way to the plot, with some nontraditional approaches to put yourself in the shoes of a male author.

After all these exercises, don't take it personally if you've developed a hand cramp by now. And hopefully your brain is so filled with information it might be time for a much-needed break.

Brain Break

INSTRUCTIONS: Flex your hands and use your imagination, because on the next page, you're going to be tasked with a new project. Don't get it twisted, you're not coloring in the brain of a Muse—remember, women don't think! Instead, use this brain to draw and color in how your male protagonist is thinking of a Muse of your choosing. Feel free to be liberal with the imagery, and if you aren't a good artist, create a color-coded key and embrace your inner Monet.

EXAMPLE: Don't worry, I've kick-started some ideas for you in the example on the right, flip the page to fill in your version.

How to make it clear the male protagonist isn't a self-insert (but he is)

 I'm writing at a café and a hot woman walked by...now I'm distracted

 Words to describe breasts that have never been used!

How the physical act of sex works

 All the women I'll fuck as a bestselling author

 Dedicated space to think about the plot

 The character arc of secondary characters

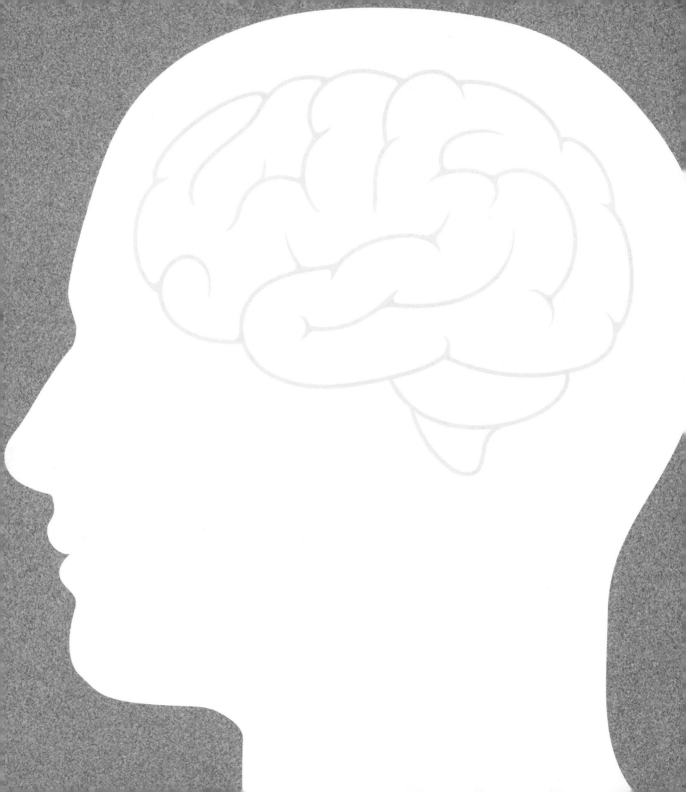

TO END ON A HIGH note, we'll put ourselves in men's shoes. Or I guess, pants. Imagining for yourself the kind of confidence that men wield on a daily basis is a kind of intoxicating high. *Imagine* the ability to go for a walk at night with noise-canceling headphones and a Janelle Monáe album blasting, going to a nightclub and staying till the wee hours of the morning without worrying about your drink, or wearing whatever you want without fear. There's a reason *cocksure* is a word—when you've got a cock to whip around, you're sure of anything. You're infallible. You aren't concerned with retribution at work for voicing an opinion or yelling back at a catcaller. You know that any medical decisions you make get to be wholly yours and that any scandals that find you won't end your career so long as you talk smoothly enough.

Which is why, for this next challenge, you need to pretend that that's *not* just a pen in your pocket. Writing women means learning to objectify them, a sacred practice that has been passed down from father to son for generations. As you've honed your skills in this book, you've practiced the fine art of objectifying women in small, everyday ways (what woman hasn't been ogled for the size of her boobs or the length of her skirt?). But now it's time to take things up a notch.

Fuck, Marry, Kill

INSTRUCTIONS: Below, examine each set of Muses and assign to them whether you'd Fuck, Marry, or Kill their character. Then provide your reasoning for each. It's not just enough to acknowledge a woman is hot, you must be able to identify what makes her worthy of the male gaze. As a writer, you must never forget that beauty is in the eye of the *male* beholder.

EXAMPLE: Nagging Wife, Virgin, Boss

FUCK: The Boss—Fucking the Boss means unlocking a fantasy that men have had since they've first entered an office. There's something about buttons straining against a white blouse and the way that calves look in a short skirt and pumps.

MARRY: The Virgin—If you marry the Virgin you're set for life. You're getting her when she's young and malleable. You can form the rest of her life: how you like to be fucked, how your laundry should be folded, and what time dinner should be on the table.

KILL: **The Nagging Wife**—Killing of the Nagging Wife is a no-brainer. Nothing's a greater turn off in life and the marriage bed than the shrill voice of a woman hounding you about daycare or groceries. Plus after all those kids, who wants to see those sagging breasts?

Secretary, Virgin, Librarian

FUCK:

MARRY:

KILL:

Whore, Matron, Nagging Wife

FUCK:

MARRY:

KILL:

Femme Fatale, Boss, Librarian

FUCK:

MARRY:

KILL:

Nagging Wife, Boss, Librarian

FUCK:

MARRY:

KILL:

Whore, Femme Fatale, Virgin

FUCK:

MARRY:

KILL:

Secretary, Boss, Matron

FUCK:

MARRY:

KILL:

Virgin, Secretary, Whore

FUCK:

MARRY:

KILL:

Now that you've shown that you can write like a male author, you must show that you can think like them too. Breaking down what makes a woman fuckable is a simple practice done in fraternities and locker rooms around the world, and while it is natural for some and hard for others, it is far from the most difficult thing you must master. Writing like a man entails thinking like one, too, and putting to use the Muses you've learned and fruits you've encountered.

Dip Your Toes in Purple Prose

INSTRUCTIONS: Using the below example as inspiration, write a passage around one of the Muses that you think is fuck-worthy. Bonus points will be given for sexual and anatomical creativity.

EXAMPLE: Logan hadn't expected to find himself in his office building lobby after the company Christmas party, waiting for the elevator to take him up to his boss's office, but here he was, nevertheless. Based on all the whiskey he'd drunk (real men only drink old-fashioneds), he was sure that there'd be a hangover in his future. But for now, he was riding that perfect wave of drunk where the world was the right amount of fuzzy.

He wasn't sure on the details of why Amanda needed to see him this late in the evening, but, as the elevator rose upward and he recalled the way trousers had hugged her figure tonight, he wasn't particularly mad about it. The elevator doors opened with a ding, and Logan headed for her office; he could see her silhouette through the glass pane of her office door, the curve of her ass as she moved acting like a homing beacon. She'd always had a body like a Coke bottle.

"Ah, Logan, thank you for making time this evening," said Amanda as Logan entered her office. Somehow she still looked put together, not a blond hair out of place and the lipstick she wore still perfectly emphasizing her sensuous, doll-like lips. "I'm sorry to pull you out of the Christmas party, but I wanted to discuss your...performance."

Logan's cock stiffened in his pants, and he could swear she noticed, the way her throat bobbed. He was sure her blouse had another button undone, too. "Of course, always happy to make time for you, Amanda."

She began talking, her fingers stroking the length of the

desk. Logan imagined it was him her delicate fingers were running the length of. He had to hold back a groan as he envisioned himself striding over to her and ripping open her blouse. He didn't think she was wearing a bra, and with the way her generous grapefruit-sized breasts strained against the buttons, he was pretty sure her nipples were as hard as marbles.

Your Turn

A Tale of Two Titties

PART III

PUSH UP

12

The Crux of the Issue

AS WE APPROACH THE CULMINATION of your journey, it is time to take your knowledge and truly apply it. If you're intimidated, that's totally natural. From our youth, we are silently told that men are the best, greatest, and default, and that women have the privilege of following in their footsteps—though we must never get too cocky. Our lives are informed by men of the past, from the very way we observe our days* named for a man to even the elements of time itself.**

And then there's the backbone of our education itself. Even the books we read in our childhood are dictated by men. Much of our childhood in the American education system is spent reading assigned books, which are always a mixed bag. Some days

* Julius Caesar is responsible for the calendar we *almost* use today, the Julian calendar. The biggest difference? Our calendars account for a leap day, though that was also introduced by a dude—Pope Gregory XIII.

** You can blame George Hudson's love of insect collecting after work hours for being the first to seriously introduce daylight saving time.

* I want to be clear that this is not the fault of teachers but the fault of our government choosing to not adequately fund schools and thus forcing teachers to provide supplies for their students themselves.

you're handed a dog-eared copy as old as your grandmother to take home, and others you're forced to read aloud from a class copy.* The United States Department of Education doesn't have a one-and-done list of required reading for middle- and high-school English classes, which allows English teachers across the country a certain amount of flexibility to teach the books they want to educate students about a certain skill. From there, it's up to the districts and teachers to select what fits for their classrooms.

But while there's no universal reading list, casual conversations with friends have them able to name a boatload of male authors, the likes of which include Ernest Hemingway, John Steinbeck, Jack London, George Orwell, and J. D. Salinger. As for female authors? There's a small handful of the same voices—Jane Austen, Margaret Atwood, S. E. Hinton, and Harper Lee. And regardless of gender, for the most part, these lists are astoundingly white. For the select few diverse voices that do make the cut, there are politicians who are actively working to remove those books from public school libraries and even just *public libraries* for no reason other than personal disagreement with the subject matter.

What this means is that the classic literary canon is largely made up of white male voices influencing the way people view the world around them. From grade school to college, we are told to look up to writers whose work is entrenched in misogyny, and seldom do we discuss it. George Orwell may write that a female character falls more in love with his protagonist, Henri, when he stabs her,* but that's not what we center our literary conversations around. Instead we focus on Orwell's adventures in poverty, his escapades, and the lessons he learns.

Down and Out in Paris and London

So when a modern male writer objectifies women in favor of an intriguing plot point, can we really blame them? If Steinbeck can write that a pregnant woman is only capable of thinking "in terms of reproduction and motherhood,"** can we really fault aspiring authors for writing women as shallow and subservient? After all, they're just following in the misogynistic footsteps of the men before them. Thanks to English teachers bending over backwards to find the meaning of the color of a curtain in a story about the meatpacking industry, every reader has become an expert at ignoring the sexism for a good plot. Evidently, including women in the stacks of assigned reading

*** The Grapes of Wrath*

147

comes at great peril—what if women think they matter? Or worse, that their voices deserve to be heard?

We have been prioritizing male writers for centuries, in everything from newspapers to fiction to scientific essays. Men have been allowed to write the feminine perspective, laws about the female body, and have even been responsible for crafting wildly misinformed articles about how the female body works. It would seem that giving women even a modicum of control, like the right to vote, comes with strings attached and an expectation that we should be grateful for anything at all. Men want to be rewarded for doing the absolute bare minimum.

After all is said and done, when men finally pick up a book by a woman, it feels like we have to throw them a ticker tape parade. That there are men who can name a female author who *isn't* J. K. Rowling, Margaret Atwood, or Jane Austen is an almost-hard-to-believe statement. There are even those who act like reading a female writer is doing the rest of us a favor.

When screenwriter Richard Curtis finally picked up books written by women during the first Covid-19 lockdown in 2019, he said he had a "genuine epiphany" and began buying books written by the likes of Anne Tyler and Elizabeth Strout not only for himself but also for his friends.* And while part of me wants to say "good for him," that he's finally educating himself after a lifetime of not reading female authors, another part of me muses on why we are acting as if this is something that deserves a pat on the back? Women have been fantastic writers for centuries. Whoopie for men just now making that discovery for themselves. Picking up a book written by a female author is well and truly the bare minimum for any reader. And to be absolutely clear, you can't argue in favor of diversifying your bookshelf if the only people you're adding to it are white women. Women of color and nonbinary individuals deserve a place on your shelf too.

It is truly astounding that we as a society continue to prioritize the words written by men hundreds of years ago over those written by women from the last five years or the last five hundred. Our scholars continue to study the dusty pages of men who were perhaps relevant for their time, and sure, can be considered classics, while ignoring the stories of and by women. Women remain shut out, and men continue to write our histories.

*The Guardian, 2022: "Books by women that every man should read: chosen by Ian McEwan, Salman Rushdie, Richard Curtis, and more."

And when there are women who manage to wiggle their way in, we seldom hear about them. Take Emily Wilson, who was the first woman to translate Homer's *Odyssey* into English. Few know who she is, fewer have read her translation, and while there are zillions of different iterations of *Odyssey*, hers takes something else into account. Women. The epic poem is one of the oldest pieces of literature typically read in schools and colleges, and that alone makes it an important part of our culture. Wilson's approach doesn't change the language to fit our idealization of women. Instead, some of Wilson's differences in translation center on how men softened and changed the language, from men referring to slaves as "nurse" or "chambermaid" to calling the weaver, Penelope's, hand "steady" instead of the actual translation which is "thick." *

* A subtle difference, perhaps, but one full of the cultural disgust for fat women.

The substitutions are subtle, and while they don't change the story itself, they change the way the story is consumed. As Wilson puts it, "Part of fighting misogyny in the current world is having a really clear sense of what the structures of thought and the structures of society are that have enabled androcentrism in different cultures, including our own." In her translation of a male-dominated text, Wilson is able straddle the line of male thought and feminine perspective to paint a more complete picture of Odysseus's experience and its impact on the women he encountered.

And all because a woman's voice was allowed to be heard.

Pulling from what you've learned along your journey through this book, it's time to take the first step into the shoes of men. Your words will be the first step infiltrating the world of men and making sure *your* voice gets to be heard. So maybe we need to adopt some of their language to do it, but we'll slither into their world regardless. As you move forward, it's OK to be intimidated, acknowledge it, and then dig within yourself and find that ember of spite.* Fuel it, grab a cup of coffee, and get to changing the narrative!

* Spite, I have found, is truly the greatest motivator. It's what inspired the creation of Men Write Women and what has fueled every word of this workbook.

A Woman's Place

PART OF WRITING A NOVEL is figuring out where exactly your characters belong. By now you've hopefully learned that an integral part of being a writer isn't really about the quality of the plot but rather the marketability. Sex and hot women sell, so if you can't think of a plot, no problem! There's a reason why porn sells, and it isn't for the storyline. But having a hot woman in your world-building doesn't mean having her as a main character. This isn't a Disney movie! In fact, in fiction as well as the real world, women belong in a select few places—and that's in a supporting role. As writers, even as we flex our fingers and create a world of fantasy with dragons and dwarves and orcs, extending our imagination to including the fairer sex is truly hitting the outer limits of what's possible.

Even hugely successful franchises like *Game of Thrones* have kept powerful women in the margins of their own stories. Sure, Daenerys is a strong young woman,* but only because she's earned that strength after a healthy dose of trauma. Similarly, the only way Sansa manages to find a place at Winterfell where she is viewed with respect, shoulder to shoulder with John, is by being emotionally and physically abused by just about every man she's encountered. Meanwhile, the men, particularly, on the show, find themselves and their heritage with sweeping travels and adventure; women are tortured and raped.

Even *Lord of the Rings* has few enough female characters that you can count them all on one hand—some of whom aren't even in the work long enough for the average person to remember their names. While the books allow for an element of feminism, the films give Éowyn the infamous line of "I am no man!" And while that ought to be a female empowerment moment, it gets lost in the weeds of a movie series that relegates its female characters to side quests where they are mooning after men. Any echo of feminism is lost, anyway, in the fact that there's not a single woman in the Fellowship...or in *The Hobbit*. No, really, there's not a single female character

* Calling her a woman is generous. In the novels, she's like fourteen—a child.

in *The Hobbit*. Which just goes to show that in history and fiction, should a woman need to be present, her only role is to uplift the man, be they a warlock or the Chosen One.

But fear not, dear reader, this extends beyond fantasy too. When crafting your plot, should you choose to have female characters, it is wisest to outline their role in advance, so you don't find yourself giving her more ink than she deserves. As you learned with the Muses, female characters at their most base contribute nothing but a lesson, which means that the women in your novel should be leveraged for exposition or character building, written with only enough depth to see them at face value but not enough that readers will want to explore their story instead.

Of course, you don't have to turn to the pages of fiction for such examples of practical application. There are still plenty of men in the real world who view women as nothing more than a uterus on legs, with the sole job of keeping house and keeping children. And it feels like more than ever, these men are proud to wear their ignorance as a badge of honor—crowing it from their social media channels or in distasteful shirts declaring their incelhood. Not long ago, a man on Twitter went viral for a particularly ignorant take. This man—we can call him Tom—shared in his Twitter bio that he'd once worked at Google and Meta (formally Facebook), and was now hacking it as an entrepreneur. In a now-deleted tweet, he said, "Women shouldn't code...perhaps be influencers/creators instead. It's their natural strength. Coding is a brutal 24/7 job, mutually exclusive with motherhood—after nine-months maternity leave, they come back obsolete and out-dated. Elon Musk even says birth rate is falling too much."

I wish I were fucking kidding. He went on to post a tirade of threaded tweets saying he wasn't discriminating, just encouraging women to stay home. Which honestly, dude, if you want to scream about that to your fifty-thousand followers, power to ya. But remember that whole "used to work at Google and Meta" bit? Turned out he'd been asked to conduct interviews for Google during his time there. The same day he tweeted that women shouldn't be coders, he tweeted out this spicy bad boy: "So when I used to conduct interview for Google, I rejected all women on the spot and trashed their resumes in front of them. I told them 'Go have some kids. Don't worry, I'm smarter than you, I know.' Then I gave them an NP-hard problem and went home."

Which brings me to my point. How is it that this dude, and

all the others who smashed the like button on that tweet, are so proud of thinking that women are meant for nothing more than motherhood? Candidly, I don't know. This book is not a deep dive into the psychological reasoning behind misogynists, so what I will say instead is that men are like rats. Where there's one [with a misogynistic opinion], there's a hundred more you can't see. Of course, these are just the men brazen enough to show their whole entire misogynistic ass; there's still plenty more who view themselves as forward-thinking feminists until it comes to decide in real life which partner needs to stay home. In that case, she who bore it...it just *makes sense* that the new mama stays home. After all, she just inherently knows how to change a diaper.* And honestly, those men are worse. When a woman is face to face with a man who is telling her her worth only extends to how many children she can have or how many pot roasts she can get on the table by six, she at least knows what she's getting into. It's the men who hide their sexism behind long-winded posts about how thankful they are for a wife who does everything at home or who test the waters with a "make me a sandwich" joke that should really scare us. If men can hide their contempt for women so easily, what else are they capable of?

* Because Daddy was too busy joining his buddies at the bar for a playoff game to go to any of the parenting classes he'd agreed to. "Oops! You can show me later, honey!"

And that's just in domestic life; being a woman in the workplace can be exhausting. Many women spend their careers being told that they just need to work a little bit harder and they'll break the glass ceiling—girlboss their way through the minefield of sexism. While the women who've paved the way for us are heroines, they also dealt with going against boy's clubs, getting trash-talked in the workplace, and having their careers undermined for simply deciding to swim against the current. Men don't have to be worried about boybossing up the corporate food chain or what will happen if they speak up in a meeting. Women are told constantly to speak quieter, to rise above, and to wait our turn all while continuously being locked out of the rooms where decisions happen. Sometimes it feels as though we spend so long changing ourselves to fit into a man's world that we find ourselves falling behind with no space to catch up, knowing they'll never slow down.

So Fuck Them

This section is about stooping so far to their level that you become one with the earthworms. And really, isn't that what a woman's place is all about? Being ground into the dirt repeatedly so that you can be fodder for the growth of a man. Why shatter a glass ceiling when you can take a side road and end up on the other side without the cuts and bruises to show for it?

Male writers would have you believe that a female character's place is behind the male protagonist, and frankly, they're right. It's just that playing second fiddle doesn't look the same in every book. Of course, it wouldn't be right to just expect you to pull these stereotypes out of thin air, and thankfully, you don't have to. As it turns out, you've already been introduced to them with the Muses.

When trying to figure out where a female character fits into a story, you'll need to begin by distilling all the traits you've given her into a nice little stereotype can be retrofitted to one of the Muses. From there, identifying the duties of a Muse is simple. The Librarian is to provide exposition and context clues while, of course, never taking away the glory of the discovery from our hero. The Nagging Wife has dinner on the table by seven and a house kept in tip-top shape for the hero to come home to, whereas the Virgin provides an element of escapism to our weary, world-travelling hero. All of these moments are but vignettes into the hero's life and serve to do nothing more than cast light on to the hero's journey. The importance of those background players is never to be mentioned; it should always be assumed that the women are just happy to be there.

If men want a woman's place to be behind them, then so be it. All the better to stab them in the back and bury their corpse.

Distilling a Woman

Earlier, you learned which features best defined a Muse and became capable of identifying which string of words best fit a certain Muse. As we discussed, finding her place in the plot begins by distilling a female character. Before you build a character for yourself, you'll practice with a ready-made passage.

INSTRUCTIONS: Read each writing sample and identify the Muse, the traits you used to recognize her, and her role to her male counterpart.

Ben recognized Martha. She'd been working at the video store for a while now, and frankly, she was hard to forget. She stood behind the counter, backlit by the neon sign, looking for all the world downright cherubic with the blue bow in her curls. Something stirred within him as he watched her twirl the sucker around in her mouth, oblivious to his gaze.

MUSE:

TRAITS:

HER ROLE:

Lois had been up for hours, and it showed. Upon greeting her at the door, Pete had immediately noticed the blue circles under her eyes and the stench of bleach she wore like perfume. "You couldn't have tried to make yourself presentable for Bob?" he hissed.

MUSE:

TRAITS:

HER ROLE:

By the time Julian got into the office, it was well past ten. He knew there was a chance he was fired, but he hurried down the hall nevertheless. Just ahead, he could see Susan, her short skirt, tights, and heels had him envisioning himself drawing the blinds in his office and bending her over his desk. Really, what were a few more minutes? Knowing Susan, she'd probably already accounted for it in his schedule anyway.

MUSE:

TRAITS:

HER ROLE:

The bar was a shithole, with dollar bills taped to the ceiling, a sticky bar top, and a fine layer of dust on all the top-shelf bottles of booze, but it was still Fred's favorite. If you'd asked him why, he would've said it was because it was the only bar that had Hamm's on tap. But really, it was because of Glen, the rather portly, rosy-cheeked bartender who sent Fred home at the end of the night with a Hamm's for the road and a Tupperware full of leftovers for his dinner.

MUSE:

TRAITS:

HER ROLE:

They were halfway through their meeting and Marvin couldn't tell if Nina was just intently focused on her computer screen or if she was checking her lipstick. He himself was focused on her lipstick—the red slash that so perfectly carved her lips from her face. It was her signature, and he'd spent many a monthly budget meeting wondering what it would be like to have those lips moaning his name instead of cursing him out.

MUSE:

TRAITS:

HER ROLE:

It was just Dan, Zella, and their boss in the briefing room now. It wasn't the first time they'd been the only two trusted on a top-secret mission, Zella there for her interrogation skills that Dan was sure had nothing to do with her steely gaze and everything to do with her preference for low-buttoned blouses and her ability to manipulate men. Dan was the weapons specialist, and looking at Zella, he was locked and loaded. Many a man had tried to hold their own bedroom interrogation session with Zella, but Dan liked to think he'd be the first to succeed.

MUSE:

TRAITS:

HER ROLE:

When Miguel had been told he'd been meeting with the archivist, he'd pictured a papery woman who could recite history from memory itself. Dr. Diana Malora was unexpected. She was tall and willowy, her hair a halo of tight black coils, and leonine eyes that didn't miss a thing. There was something sensual in the way that she rolled a pencil in her fingers that made his heart flutter. Of course, it didn't hurt that she was the only person in the country who could read this era of cuneiform.

MUSE:

TRAITS:

HER ROLE:

The pounding hangover that Dewey woke up with a strong reminder of the night before. He had only the vaguest idea of how he'd gotten home. The last thing he could remember was burying his face in a pair of tits that were most definitely fake and that reeked of cigarette smoke, a ringed hand closing a cab door for him, and the husky voice of a woman saying his cock wasn't worth her life.

MUSE:

TRAITS:

HER ROLE:

14

The Role She Plays

REGARDLESS OF WHERE A FEMALE character is inserted, it's important that even her background or origin story is told from a male perspective. Art imitates life, and in reality, women are rarely allowed to tell their own stories; hell, during Shakespeare's era, women weren't even allowed to don a cloak and pretend to *be* a female character. Men in film and fiction are like an invasive species—once an idea has been planted involving a man, they suddenly take over the entire story. *Hidden Figures*, the book and later film adaptation, tells the story of Katherine Johnson, one of the first Black NASA scientists and the NASA mathematician who calculated the trajectory for getting the first American into space.* She was a behemoth in her own right,

*Alan Shepherd, May 5 1961.

with a mind capable of crushing numbers at a mind-boggling speed and advancing space travel in a way that would make Isaac Asimov jealous, but readers and viewers observed that the obstacles she faced went far outside the realm of space.

Racism was still abundant at NASA, and the film adaptation of *Hidden Figures* capitalizes this. But instead of showing how racism affected Johnson—there was only a Whites Only bathroom in her building, but she used it anyway, and she wasn't allowed into Mission Control to watch the launch she was instrumental for—director Theodore Melfi rewrites history. He fictionalizes a composite, white, male character to act as Johnson's boss, played by Kevin Costner. Costner's character acts as the figurehead battling NASA's racism; he destroys the Colored Ladies Only bathroom sign, he breaks with tradition and allows Johnson into Mission Control.

In a story *about* Katherine Johnson, a white dude *who wasn't even real* gets to shine. And while *Hidden Figures* is a horrific example, it's far from the only one. Men have been dominating the female experience for lifetimes. Nathaniel Hawthorne writes about the impact of a Puritanical culture on a young woman who is pregnant out of wedlock in *The Scarlett Letter*, a novel that is still taught in schools because, as we all know, there were no women who wrote about their experience in that period. In *Titanic*, Rose is finally able to take ownership over her life—it's just a shame every decision she makes is dictated by Jack. By the time she gets on the research vessel, her whole life since the sinking of the ship has been lived in the shadow of a dead man. Even her decision to damn the Heart of the Ocean to the depths of the ocean are driven by Jack in his watery grave—because God forbid she let her granddaughter have a legacy or a small fortune to live off of.

And with everything, even fiction has a piece of reality in it. In the real world, it's not unusual to see a panel of all-male doctors discussing the symptoms and treatment of endometriosis. The irony that male doctors often don't listen to women's pain, or that they blame it on weight or stress, is not lost on me. In fiction and reality, men overlook and overwrite women, and it impacts almost every facet of our lives.

Our Bodies Are Not Our Own

Considering most men can't find the clit much less the uterus, I find it fascinating that many have taken it upon themselves to dictate whether or not women should be able to decide if they want to bear children. If we're just dictating shit as we see fit, I'd like to announce that I think that no man should be allowed to make a decision about any woman's body unless he's been able to make one cum once, and evidence must be provided. The question of who has the right to someone's body seems to only pertain to women. It's something that comes up in rape cases and abortion cases, and even conversations about trans people, and is propelled forward in the media by men owning the stories about women. Stories about women, be they in *Time* or in a fiction novel, seldom ignore her body or what she looks like, even if the story is about activism or intellect. This right of ownership, for men at a club to assume it's OK to grope a woman who is scantily clad, has infiltrated even our political and healthcare systems.

When the initial draft majority opinion on *Roe v. Wade* from the Supreme Court was first leaked, the country was in uproar. Women believed their rights were being taken away, and the Supreme Court was disturbed that their privacy was violated.* So while Supreme Court justices ruled in astounding speed the sanctity of their homes, women began to search in

* The irony of this is...not lost on me. That SCOTUS judges think that getting further up inside my uterus than an IUD is well and good but a leaked piece of paper is an invasion of privacy is mind-boggling. Anyway, donate to your local abortion provider. The five judges behind the opinion draft are sitting in public positions of power but get their chastity belts in a twist when protestors show up at their homes as if they haven't been more involved in my sex life than past boyfriends.

earnest for ways to protect their bodies from unwanted children. Google searches for terms like *tubal ligation*, at-home *abortion*, and *misoprostol* surged in the days following the official reversal.*

Tubal ligation surgical procedure is also known as female sterilization, and it involves blocking or cutting the fallopian tubes in order to prevent pregnancy. This procedure is permanent, and for women concerned they may not be able to get birth control, and adamant that children were not for them, a viable option. With growing knowledge that Plan B can expire, and IUDs only last so long, tubal ligation was, and continues to be, one of the few remaining ways for a person with a uterus to take full control over their own body. Especially in a world where it seems that neither political party gives a shit about making abortions legal and attainable.

However, as women sought out options for tubal ligations, more and more found themselves taking to the internet with stories of being told no from their doctors. Doctors were telling women that in order for them to perform a tubal ligation, hoops would need to be jumped through. Tales on news sites and social platforms were a dime a dozen as

* Other than at the end of June 2022, *tubal ligation* was searched for the most September 23–29, 2018. It was during this time that Christine Blasey Ford testified before the Supreme Judiciary Committee in regard to her accusation of then–Supreme Court nominee Brett Kavanaugh sexually assaulting her. During his hearing, Kavanaugh had already been cagey in answering questions centered on abortion. For many women, the way he spoke about Blasey Ford and the reception of his testimony by Republicans was confirmation of something else. First, he was almost certain to be confirmed. Second, rapists are everywhere, and so long as they are white and male, they will never face repercussions.

women shared how they were told by *medical professionals* that the only way their doctor would be willing to perform this procedure would be if they hit a certain age or if their husband gave approval. Vasectomies can be gotten for a song, but God forbid a woman decide to take her tubes and reproductive freedom by the reins.

With so many doctors inserting themselves into a woman's right to choose, long-standing groups on Facebook and Reddit began to grow, detailing which doctors would grant sterilization in a specific city, how to ask for sterilization, conversations to have with your insurance company, and how to talk to your partner. When women can't get answers from their doctor, they turn to each other. In *Jurassic Park*, Michael Crichton said that "life finds a way," but I'd argue that "life" is an oversimplification. It's *women* who have fought tooth and nail to find a way.

Fiction is rooted in reality more often than we'd like to believe. Don't believe me?

Fiction or Politician

INSTRUCTIONS: See if you can tell which of the passages below is from fiction and which was said by an American politician:

1. "Why do we have laws in place that protect the eggs of a sea turtle or the eggs of eagles? Because, when you destroy an egg, you're killing a preborn baby sea turtle or preborn baby eagle. Yet when it comes to a preborn human baby, rather than a sea turtle, that baby will be stripped of all protections in all fifty states..."

WHICH?　AUTHOR　POLITICIAN

2. "Nine times out of ten, if a girl gets raped, it's at least partly her own fault. The tenth time—well, alright."

WHICH?　AUTHOR　POLITICIAN

3. "Keep sex drive all bottled up inside and you get dull-witted. Throws your whole body out of whack. Holds the same for men and women. But with a woman, her monthly cycle can get irregular, and when her cycle goes off, it can make her imbalanced."

WHICH?　AUTHOR　POLITICIAN

4. "If you have [silicone breast implants] you're healthier than if you don't. That is what the ultimate science shows…"

WHICH?　AUTHOR　POLITICIAN

5. "…the female body always looks its best when it is flat on its back, stretched out, the tummy pulled flat, the breasts naturally upright without the vertical drag of gravity to pull them down.

WHICH?　AUTHOR　POLITICIAN

6. "If it's a legitimate rape, the female body has ways to shut that whole thing down."

WHICH? | AUTHOR | POLITICIAN

7. "Can this same procedure then be done in a pregnancy? Swallowing a camera and helping the doctor determine what the situation is?"

WHICH? | AUTHOR | POLITICIAN

8. "[Pregnancy] was paradoxical in that only the female of the species could perform the amazing feat, while perhaps being less psychologically prepared for it than male would have been. No woman enjoys the sight of sagging breasts and a bulging stomach, no matter how maternal her urge."

WHICH? | AUTHOR | POLITICIAN

If you're concerned that you can't *quuuiiiite* tell the difference, you're not alone. I roast male writers for their inability to write women as human, but it's not as if they're the only ones who view women as essentially subhuman. Congressmen, presidents, and world leaders have looked at women as pawns since we first emerged from the quagmires of evolution. And if creationism is more your vibe, take a look at Eve. Adam is made from dust, Eve from Adam's rib cage. She truly is not her own person. And when the two of them eat the forbidden fruit, she is punished with childbirth and submitting to man while Adam is charged with a little sweat equity.[*] And thus thousands of years of subservience has been granted unto women, with crusty-ass congressmen and male authors continuing the tradition.

So where does that land us now?

It means that the women you write should be written in the image of your male protagonist. In the solar system of your novel, your protagonist is the sun, and the women in your book simply revolve around him. For every action the protagonist takes, the ripple effect should be felt by every female character. Our place in the shadow of man is literally biblical, but

[*] I'll admit that I'm summarizing here. Genesis 3:17–3:19 says to Adam: "Cursed is the ground because of you; through painful toil you will eat food from it all the days of your life. It will produce thorns and thistles for you, and you will eat the plants of the field. By the sweat of your brow you will eat your food until you return to the ground, since you were taken; for dust you are and to dust you will return."

nobody talks about how quickly a shadow can open its maw and become an abyss to fall into, and when the men fumble, we'll eat them right up.

To ensure that you fully understand a woman's place, I've crafted a handy test of your situational awareness. Much like a Hitchcock movie, there are several tried-and-true scenarios by which women characters might enter into a story. From the classic coffee shop meet-cute to the sexy reveal of taking off a pair of glasses, female characters exist to help the main (male) character get what he wants. What Mr. Man needs, Mr. Man gets. Writers must be willing to ask themselves: *What does my male character need, and how can she help get him there?*

Another Match Play

INSTRUCTIONS: Match the action to the need to prove the following statement true: When a man needs _____, the woman must _____.

When a Man Needs _____
the Woman Must _____

to show his intelligence •

• require saving from impending doom

to display he's learned from his actions •

• act clueless in her area of expertise

to establish himself as physically strong •

• always behave as the perfect romantic partner (no matter what happens)

to explain the plot or the world •

• be overly emotional

to be shown as unshakeable •

• make nonsensical decisions

THE GUIDELINES COVERED SO FAR apply equally to literary fiction, fantasy, detective stories, and so much more—but now it's time to encourage aspiring writers to get specific, finding their niche and honing their craft in the context of a chosen genre. Figuring out your niche need not be a painful process. You can either go with whichever one calls to you or simply pick one at random. And once you find a plot that resonates with you, just rinse and repeat. It's worked for Nicholas Sparks and Dan Brown! You can't tell me that you could name the specific book if I simply described "handsome, bookish man goes on a historical treasure hunt and, along the way, meets a gorgeous, smart woman who helps him."

Of course, it isn't as easy as hooking up with a sorority girl on rush night; it requires some strategy. But fear not, I've taken all the guesswork out of it, and instead made it a game anyone can play!

The Genre Detour is the perfect place to get your bearings and see how, based on your decisions, female characters fit into your plot. Using the map on the following page, find your way to your genre.

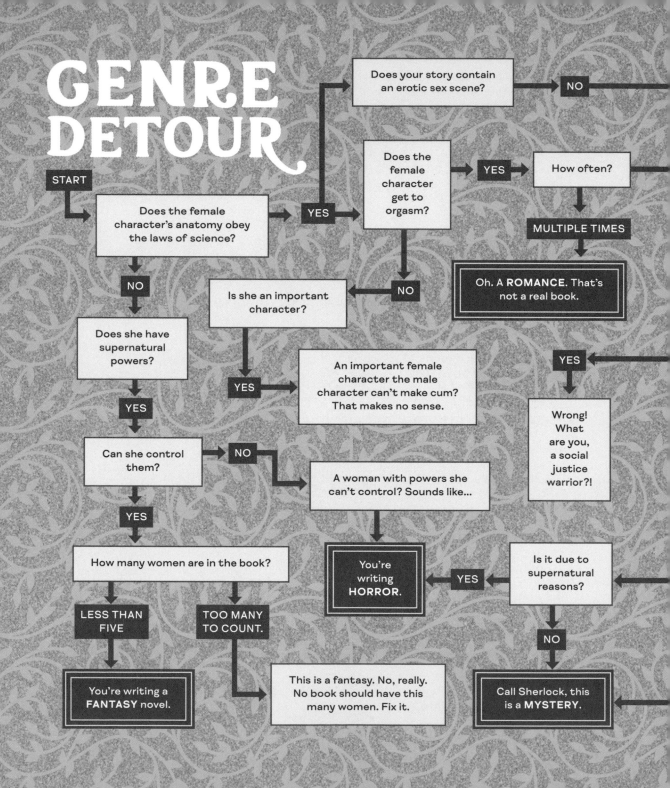

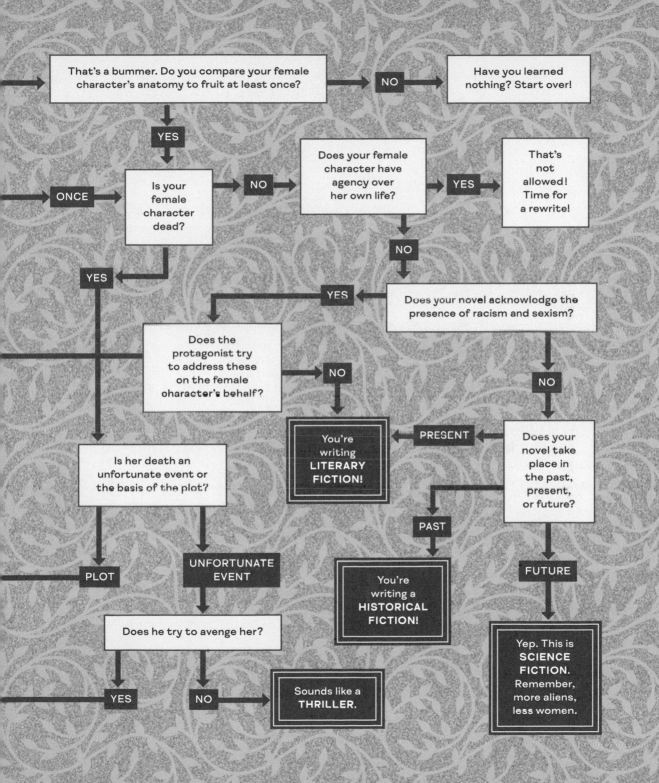

As you can see, the Genre Detour covers the Seven Basic Genres.[*] plus Romance. Romance books, as we all know, are not real books..[**] They're fluffy and smutty, and no writer worth their salt would spend their time crafting a romance book. This, of course, is due in part to the fact that romance books are for women only, and they wouldn't know a smart plot line if it gave them a roguish wink.

You'll notice that two genres are not present—Classics, and Comics. Let's address that. Classics are not something you just write; they are made carefully and with many marketing dollars. If you truly feel like writing like one of the Classics, I suggest you go use their tried-and-true method of "paid by the word, very racist, stolen from someone else."

As for Comics, well, we'll save that for later. While not perhaps traditionally considered true fiction, they've certainly found their chokehold in the world. It's just such a bummer that so many of the heavy-hitter comics, like Marvel and DC, feel the need to write and illustrate "strong female characters" like they just waltzed out of their spank bank. Even more frustrating, when women ask for characters that have a modicum of realism,[***] male readers get up in arms over the "woke

[*] They're like the Seven Deadly Sins in that everyone seems to identify with one or theother and the rest of humanity think that that makes them evil.

[**] Never mind that romance books continue to flourish, topping 47 *million* books sold from March 2020 to March 2021.

[***] Listen I want to give Catwoman the benefit of the doubt, but I don't believe for a minute that she's cartwheeling across rooftops in a rubber suit that offers her above-average-sized breasts all the support of a painter's tape. Don't even get me started on the poses that aren't anatomically possible for even the most hypermobile individuals.

police." While more and more women show up to conventions and superhero movies, male fans, directors, and writers continue to sweep their fandom under the rug in favor of continuing stereotypical portrayals. I could continue to wax poetic about comics, but I'll save that for another book.

When we talk about fiction, each genre has its own set of rules and classic plot points. Now that you have a general feel for what genre your book fits into, it's time to refine that concept to make sure it can truly go toe to toe with the John Grishams of the world. Who knows, if you're lucky, you too can have a whole team of writers writing your books for you!

The Magic Penis Mandate

Before we delve too far into the world of genres and their rules, the Magic Penis Mandate needs to be introduced. A concept as old as time, the Magic Penis Mandate is a rule that umbrellas over all genres. While you have never heard its formal name before, I assure you that you are *intimately* familiar with the Mandate and the impact it can have on women, fictional and real alike. In short, the Magic Penis Mandate is a universal idea rooted in male pleasure, which, as we all know, is the root of everything in this world. As Benjamin Franklin probably meant to put it, "Nothing is certain but male orgasms, death, and taxes."

What the Mandate means in application, though, is that all men think they're God's gift to women. For fictional characters, it's the ability to make a woman cum in two seconds flat. For the authors themselves, it's writing female anatomy as if it's an all-you-can-eat buffet. As Chip Cheek so delicately put it in his novel *Cape May*:*

"And in answer he freed her from her underwear, spread her legs and opened her with his tongue: a soft, soft bursting, warm and smoothly wet, like olive oil. The baffling folds of skin. A scent, mostly, of Dial soap."

The Magic Penis Mandate dictates that any sexual intercourse with a male protagonist is destined to be amazing. Not only will he always get off, but he'll also see stars, and his universe will implode from the sheer amazingness of his own cock. But as for the female character? Only female characters who matter to the plot will be blessed with an orgasm. Can he make her cum? Yes, of course—he has a magic dick, after all. But does she *deserve it?* Well, that remains to be seen.

* This novel was Cheek's first, and it scored him a publishing advance of $800,000. No, that's not a typo. Someone literally paid high six figures for a book containing this passage.

And if you've learned one thing throughout this workbook let it be this: just because it happens in a book doesn't mean there isn't truth to it. Our movies and books and TV shows continuously show us that no matter how brief, weird, or strangely positioned sex is, sex with the leading man is *always hot*. The female characters are moaning and writhing and *oh, baby*ing their way to an orgasm after a mere two minutes of sex. When you stop and think about it, it's fucked up, but not shocking. Heterosexual relationships consistently prioritize male pleasure over female pleasure, with women consistently faking an orgasm to either hasten the act or make their male partner feel good.

Chip Cheek's *Cape May* is described as a novel about "marriage, love, and sexuality and the lifelong repercussions that meeting a group of debauched cosmopolitans has on a new marriage," yet somehow, while the male protagonist Henry is fucking his way through a beach town, we never once read about his female partner's orgasming. Instead we're treated to long-winded sentences about Henry's orgasms like "long waves" or "the sun breaking through the clouds." Intentional or not, the lack of female orgasm in *Cape May* echoes it in real life too. Turns out that the orgasm gap is a real thing. Because yeah, who knew that there were real-world repercussions from things normalized in pop culture?

Numerous studies cite that, in heterosexual sex, women orgasm substantially less than men do; a cycle that persists the more couples are intimate and the less women orgasm. And while men may gasp at the discovery that, no, women do not cum every time they fuck, it really shouldn't be new information considering that 30 percent of men in a study by Durex said that they thought that helping a woman orgasm was best done through penetrative sex while over half of the women in the study said that clitoral stimulation helped them finish.

It seems believable that a general lack of anatomical knowledge is at least partially to blame. I argue, too, that some of it comes down to a lack of respect for women, our bodies, and our pleasure. Straight men act as if making a woman orgasm is hard, then turn around and have a meltdown of nuclear proportions if asked to introduce a vibrator to bed. Oh your *manhood* is offended by a vibrating piece of silicon? I'm *so sorry I wanted to cum.*

Real men can't respect the need for a female orgasm, and

fictional men* can't respect the anatomy itself. Think I'm joking? Let's explore a real-life, actually published novel and see if you've been adequately keeping up. Circle the below words that are used to describe female anatomy in E. L. Doctorow's *The Book of Daniel*

VAT	ISLAND RANGES
VIRTUE	MOTHERHOOD
VINCIBLES	VACUUM
BUTTER TUB	GLAND FORMATIONS

I hate to be the one to tell you this, but that was a trick question. Every single one of those words came from one glorious run-on sentence. How can I expect a man to make a woman cum when he's crafting a sentence that describes some part of her body as "that geology of gland formations, Stalinites and Trotskyites, the Stalinites grow down from the top, the Trotskyites up from the bottom..."?**

All of which brings us back to the Magic Penis Mandate. Whether your protagonist is fucking your female character missionary style or in a way that's only ever been seen in porn,

* I may say "fictional men" here, but to be clear, it's usually the male authors themselves. Sure there's an occasional allowance to be made for a character being a misogynistic idiot, but that's usually a pathetic excuse for an author getting caught in the cross-hairs of their own creation. And if they're ballsy enough to put their ignorance out in the wild so publicly, there's little doubt in my mind that they can tell a vulva from a Volvo.

** I have no fucking clue what part of her body this is meant to be, and frankly I'm too afraid to ask.

you must always remember that, sure, he may have the *ability* to make her cum, but the blessing of an orgasm can only appear if she deserves it. This is also an adequate opportunity to consider the Muses. The Femme Fatale probably deserves an orgasm, but a Nagging Wife? Not so much. This mandate transcends genre and can be found anywhere from horror to historical fiction.

But how to tell if the female character has been blessed with the ability to orgasm? Well, that's no small feat, but thankfully, it isn't something you have to decide alone. When you're looking for guidance, you need only consider the O Objective.

The O Objective

* What a joke; *real men* don't need foreplay.

The journey from foreplay* to climax is one fraught with peril, and the decision of who ultimately makes it to the top lies solely with the male protagonist. As a writer, it can be difficult to figure out if it's worth including an element of inclusivity by having your female character orgasm. To help you address this pickle, I'd like to introduce you to the O Objective.

In short, this ruling is set in place to ensure that you don't allow too many female characters the opportunity to orgasm. Handing out orgasms like Halloween candy is no good for anybody—firstly, it shows a reader that orgasms are easy to come by, and secondly, it tells readers that every woman should be orgasming themselves. That's a type of equality we simply don't need in this universe.

Generally speaking, unless you're writing a romance or your male protagonist's story hinges on being a romance, there should never be more orgasms than female characters in any novel. Too many orgasms throw off the whole equilibrium and introduces the potential of equal-opportunity orgasmers. You're writing a novel, not an orgy.

Which brings us to who gets actually finish.* Goody two-shoes, virgins, and bitches never orgasm. Either they're too uptight or too inexperienced, operating under the assumption that an orgasm is a mystical thing or an exotic kind of flower. Really, when it comes down to it, the only women who should be reaching a climax are either sluts who know how to fuck** or the gorgeous, dainty love interest who is rendered breathless with her first ever toe-curling experience.

* Noting, of course, that the male protagonist *always* gets to cum.

** And if we're being honest, are having sex more for the fun of it since they know it'd be faster and easier to get off with the Clit Sucker 3000.

191

Most importantly, the inability to orgasm is never the fault of the male protagonist, but rather, it rests squarely on the woman's shoulders. After all, as you've learned, there's no real science to making a woman cum, so why should anyone devote time to it? Women who *are* granted the experience must always express their sincere gratitude to the hero for bringing them to climax out of the goodness of his own heart. Sex with the hero should consistently be some of, if not *the*, best sex they've ever had in their life—something they express regularly and with fervor.

Tackling orgasms in a novel is not for the faint of heart; it's a task that truly requires grace and sensitivity. If the orgasms are too plentiful or too easy, people will start getting the idea that *everyone* should be having them, and that just sets unrealistic expectations for real-world men—who can't be expected to deliver *every* time! A good writer should treat orgasms like diamonds. It isn't that they're actually rare and hard to come by; it's just that they can be a pain in the ass to get to, and to make a woman feel *truly* special, marketing it as one of a kind puts the woman who gets them in another social class. Above all, what's most important to remember is that orgasming is a privilege, not a right.

the ORACLE of O

TAMMY LYNN—Wrinkled and freckled with sun spots, hangs around the local dive bar so often that she gets mistaken for the owner. Swears and smokes as much as the men.

ORGASM? | YES | NO | WHY?

NAOMI—A college drop-out who could pass the bar if she wanted but just has never had the motivation. She has long dark hair and sports glasses that make her look owl-eyed; she drinks whiskey and spouts philosophy.

ORGASM? | YES | NO | WHY?

MINDY—A slim, Pilates-attending, Type A party planner, she refuses to do anything unless it can be done to her exact parameters. Exclusively wears athleisure that accentuates her toned calves.

ORGASM? | YES | NO | WHY?

BRENDA—Won the Miss USA pageant for her state and Miss Congeniality at the national level, and she's training to be an orthopedic surgeon. She loves green juices and receiving flowers from the protagonist.

ORGASM? | YES | NO | WHY?

MEREDITH—Currently working as a secretary, no one knows her secret, which is that she paid for college and breast implants by working as a stripper. She still catches the eye of the executives in the office, but she's focused on keeping her nose clean.

ORGASM? | YES | NO | WHY?

AUDREY—A kindergarten teacher who, though currently single, dreams of being a stay-at-home mom of three, driving her children to school in a newly waxed Range Rover.

ORGASM? | YES | NO | WHY?

KRISTIN—Recently moved to New York City from Oklahoma City, she doesn't understand why people give her dirty looks for smiling at them on the A train. A Midwestern kind of pretty with big blue eyes, freckles, and cornsilk-colored hair.

ORGASM? | YES | NO | WHY?

CASSIDY—An executive assistant who believes in dotting every *i* and crossing every *t*. She's never once run a stop sign or gotten a speeding ticket, always tips 25 percent, and always folds the laundry the minute it's done from the dryer.

ORGASM? | YES | NO | WHY?

JOYCE—Amazonian tall with coppery red hair and green eyes, she has *finally* said yes to a date with the male protagonist. She works as a pediatric nurse at the local hospital and always carries an emergency first-aid kit in her purse.

ORGASM? | YES | NO | WHY?

KIMBERLEIGH—A work-from-home mom who sells essential oils and has a standing appointment at the local hair salon. She's the queen bee of her small town and tells everyone that she refuses to go to the city because it's dirty and dangerous.

ORGASM? | YES | NO | WHY?

Writing rationale for whether or not these women have earned an orgasm will prepare you for writing any kind of woman who meets your male protagonist. Sex can never be far from the hero's mind,[*] and every woman he meets has the potential to be his next sexual partner. Every woman wants him, but whether or not she gets his whole package is up for debate. As you pen the next great American novel, the Oracle of O should sit on one shoulder and the Magic Penis Mandate on the other; they must be applied in equal weight, or your story may lean too far into Romance territory, and we simply can't have that.

[*] Handsome or not, every male protagonist is a sex symbol in his own right, for no other reason than that he's the main character and has a penis.

15

The Genre Jaunt

EVERY GENRE HAS SOMETHING THAT makes it especially unique. As you learned in the Genre Detour, every decision you make leads you one step further down a predetermined path. Along each path, you'll encounter tropes. Wholly unavoidable, it's important to know that *trope* isn't a dirty word; applied well, it can be the seal of approval for readers to know, with certainty, that they'll love a novel. Each genre has its own flavor of tropes, which can make or break a novel. Of course, no matter how far you go down a rabbit hole, your Muses will always be there with you. Women don't break stereotypes; they *are* stereotypes.

The women in your book must play by the rules of these tropes to make the story believable, and since you are but a budding writer, you can't be expected to know all of them. But fear not, I'm here to guide you.

The Final Frontier

Science fiction. Where new worlds, cultures, and languages can come to life...but gender tropes are steadfast. In November 2021, the *New York Times* posted an article called "How H. G. Wells Predicted the Twentieth Century," the article itself is a nauseating homage to Wells, but the tweet that the *Times* sent out about the article was worse. It read: "With Jules Verne and the publisher Hugo Gernsback, H. G. Wells invented the genre of science fiction."

Mary Shelley would like a word. After all, it's her 1818 novel *Frankenstein* that far precedes any works by Verne, Gernsback, or Wells. I'd say it's insulting to write women out of history, but really, it's just par for the course. This is why it's so important to center maleness in every science fiction story. Your Muses still exist, but this time they're dressed in a form-fitting space-suit. For instance, while you might have the Boss, she's really Commander Cunt, and instead of lipstick she sports a buzz cut and sexy scar.

Science fiction may have tropes that supersede time, but it is not so backwards as to assume women can't be in leadership. It's just that, well, it shouldn't be the norm. After all, "Any official might be a woman. The Secretary-General might be a woman. There were women on the police force, even a woman with the rank of captain. It was just that, without warning, one didn't expect it in any given case." *

* *The Robots of Dawn*, Isaac Asimov

Introduce too many female leaders into your story, and your readers might start believing that that's feasible. You have to lean into the fact that women haven't earned a seat at the table, what with them being so behind the curve in the genre itself. And thus Commander Cunt is born. She's a ballsy leader, fierce, and protective of her troops. But, nevertheless, she *is* a woman. Shortly after the above line, Asimov goes on to write that the only thing that gave away the official's gender were her breasts, "the prominence of which she made no attempt to hide."

I guess even in space women have to weaponize their sexuality to make it to the top.

That being said, science fiction is still, well, fiction. Which means that, as a writer, it's your duty to pull metaphors out of

* This was Milan Kundera.

** Asimov, once again. I'd say I'm surprised, but unfortunately this man was a world classcreep in real life and between the pages of his made-up worlds.

your ass, and you don't even have to worry if it'll make sense! If you want to call a vagina a portal, do it! * You can blast off into a whole new genre filled with people who are more inclined to care about the maximum speed of a spacepod than whether or not it makes sense to have a whole scene laying out the effects of low gravity on a woman's breasts. **

PROMPT: Test your skills by describing your own Commander Cunt in the space below:

_____

_____

_____

_____

_____

_____

_____

_____

_____

_____

Final Girls

* The term "Final Girl" was coined by film critic Carol Clover, and today it is referenced in film, fiction, and TV shows.

If there's one person to get attached to while reading a thriller or mystery, it's a Final Girl.* She is the last one standing in a field of bloody corpses—battered, bruised, but still beautiful. For a trope-filled trap, turn to thrillers, wickedly fast page-turners that are blood-soaked romps through every stereotype you could imagine. The type of the cop who is tasked with solving the murder dictates just how sexist and racist the novel will be.

If it's a young, female rookie, she'll be a kind respite against a tidal wave of sexism and racism. She'll be pitted against all the other cops, who don't take her seriously due to her age and her femininity, and she'll more than likely be the only one that takes the pursuit of justice in a hard case seriously. A grizzled cop will trust no one, and his encounter with a female victim will be his first realization in his entire life that oh shit, sexism is real.** That a victim had a life outside of the crime scene never seems to resonate with them until it hits home.

When describing these female victims, even in death, it's OK—no, *preferred*—to continue to objectify them. Take a note from Haruki Murakami's *The Commodore*; when the narrator's sister dies, he goes to see her dead body, where he laments,

"Her developing breasts would never grow." One could argue that there are more poetic ways to note that his sister is dead and will never grow old(er), but why be poetic when you talk about *titties*. Murakami isn't alone in this either. Jo Nesbø, a successful Norwegian crime writer, is known for describing his female characters with a healthy dollop of horniness. In his novel *The Devil's Star,* he describes multiple deceased women by whether or not they're attractive, walking the reader through each woman's figure and attire, tying her worth in death to her beauty (or lack thereof) in life.

In order to echo these male writers, you must ignore every ounce of commonsense you possess. Thrust your female characters down a dark and dangerous alley, send them home with the suspicious stranger at the bar, allow them to walk themselves home. When writing mysteries and thrillers, nothing matters so much as the way she will ultimately be murdered. You need to put more thought into how her blood will splash against the floor and the phallic item that will be used to murder her than the decisions that she makes to lead her where she is.

In these books it doesn't matter who she is; it matters that she's dead.

** And while fiction is, well fiction, this line of thinking trends a little too close to reality for me. There are far too many men who don't take a woman's issue seriously until it impacts them at home. For some men, it can take having a girlfriend, wife, or daughter to realize that rape or domestic violence or *basic human rights* are a legitimate issue that women deal with on a day-to-day basis. The logic behind statements of, "As a brother/husband/father..." are disturbing because it doesn't give women autonomy as humans, it instead shows that these men view the women in their life as extensions of themselves that only matter when a man enters into their life and take ownership. I don't want to have access to an abortion or *justice* simply because I am, in some way, tied to a man.

* We being
Americans. The
propaganda may
pretend that this
country is the land of
the free and the home
of the brave, but that
only applies if you're
a wealthy white guy.
It seems like every
year is just another
attempt to see how
much we can fuck up
our laws and land for
the future generation.
Bodily autonomy and
a sustainable future?
Not under my roof!

INSTRUCTIONS: In thrillers and mysteries, we[*]
care most about how a woman looks when she
is a corpse. Using the space on this spread, describe
the body of a dead woman at the scene of a crime, then
draw in her sexy corpse.

This is the Way It's Always Been

Ah, historical fiction. Nothing like a quick jaunt into the past to be reminded that nothing has changed as much as we think it has. Swap out corsets for underwire bras, and you're halfway there already! Shit, in some places, women had far more rights than we do right now. Historical fiction as a whole usually revolves around two types of women who are, unsurprisingly, derivatives of our Muses. The women are either strong or demure, with their strength usually being obtained through some absolutely horrific event that, while traumatic at the time, they are written as grateful for years down the road. Demure women are sometimes pitiful and other times the ideal for all a woman should be. Headstrong women don't belong in history, because history can only be made by men.

The best part of any historical fiction is its ability to simply paint over, well, anything that is unseemly. Menstrual bleeding? Nonexistent. The cramps that came with them? A thing of legends. But the glory of dying in childbirth? Now that's as real as you or I. Women in historical fiction do the bidding of men, and that includes bearing their children, even if it kills them.

This genre of book radiates the truth behind the patriarchy.

Women are meant to be nothing more than child bearers, responsible for respawning the population. The death of the child, its sickness, or, God forbid, the child being born a girl, now all that falls on the woman. Women have been beheaded for less. The glory of a child, that credit is due to the father, whose almighty sperm were somehow supercharged for success. History is full of winners and losers, but why does it feel like the losers are almost always women?

When writing your historical fiction, it's of the utmost importance to ensure the events that occur within your pages are realistic and believable. This will require you to always keep men in mind, to give credit to men, and to note that even the victories accomplished by the female characters be duly given to the men that surround them.

There's a Reason They Call it HIStory

INSTRUCTIONS: The next spread contains achievements real women accomplished as well as the people who took credit for them. In the space beneath each statement, write a few sentences to describe how and why the woman shouldn't be given credit.

ELIZABETH MAGIE invented a board game called "The Landlord's Game" meant to show the negative impact of real-life monopolies. Roughly thirty years later, Charles Darrow would pitch and sell his game, called Monopoly, to the Parker Brothers, making him a millionaire. Magie was eventually paid around $500 for her game's patent.

Edward Pickering took credit for developing the science behind identifying how far away from Earth a star was based on its brightness by publishing the findings under his name. In reality, the idea came from **HENRIETTA LEAVITT**, and it allowed for an entirely new way for scientists to explore the universe. Even after her death, she was not credited, with scientist Harlow Shapley saying that her work was simply the foundation for his better, more important discoveries.

Scientist **EUNICE FOOTE** wasn't allowed to present her paper on the sun's effects on different gases due to her gender. Three years later, John Tyndall, an Irish physicist published a paper about a similar effect. It's he who is credited with discovering the greenhouse effect.

Theoretical physicists **TSUNG DAO LEE** and **CHEN NING YANG** won a Nobel Prize in Physics in 1957 for their theory disproving the law of parity during beta decay. However, physicist **CHIEN SHIUNG WU'S** work was never acknowledged, even though it was her experiments which proved their theory true.

A famous line in literature goes, "I hope she'll be a fool—that's the best thing a girl can be in this world, a beautiful little fool." If it sounds familiar, it's because it's from F. Scott Fitzgerald's *The Great Gatsby*. Shame it's not actually his line, though, as it was actually said by his wife, **ZELDA**, after their daughter was born.

The Last Gasp of Relevancy

Nothing makes my eyes roll further in the back of my head than literary fiction by a white dude. A genre that's focused more on characters than on plot, literary fiction often feels like a self-insert for a guy who never got a date to prom. Usually centered on a plot that has as much substance as rice paper, literary fiction challenges the author to fulfill his wildest dreams whilst not paying any attention to the world around him in the hopes of making some sort of ambiguous point.

How that point is made is unimportant, and the details surrounding the journey to said point are murky. Never mind that a reader might get caught up on some of those points, like, for instance, the anatomical impossibility of saying the female character could "feel his swollen crown somewhere near her heart" in a book about the morality of social media.[*] How she is fucked is less important than the fact that she is being fucked. As you've been taught, anatomical specificities don't matter in any genre, but none more so than science fiction and literary fiction.

One could say that Richard Powers's passage about his female character beginning to climax while soaping up an

The Circle, David Eggers

212

ugly wound in her leg is odd, but a real author knows that in reality it's commentary on the physical manifestation of the emotional pain that results from divorce.* A novel about trees and the human impact on the world around us, Powers is the poster child for literary fiction, enjoying flexing his linguistic prowess with phrases like "tits glowing like precious pearls" and "gelid air strokes her like a sex toy." While these may seem outrageous and florid, writers who truly embrace the way of literary fiction can gain fame, fortune, and more awards than they can name.

If a wince-worthy sentence makes you question if the male author has ever met a woman, you're on the right track to being pinnacle of literary fiction. No need for it to make sense when the sole goal is introspection!

INSTRUCTIONS: In order to try your hand at literary fiction, you will be given a short sentence to expand upon. However you see fit, your goal is to make a longer passage that may not connect to the plot, but will connect to the reader. Of course, don't forget that, even though you're writing in the realm of literary fiction, the rules you've learned thus far still apply.

* To be clear, I absolutely am bullshitting you. I have absolutely no idea what Powers is getting at in *The Overstory* in this scene, other than making clear that he's never made a woman cum. If he had, he'd know there needs to be (or should be) an iota of foreplay that exists beyond fondling a leg wound.

213

Lola's dress was short. _____

_____

_____

_____

_____

_____

Sarah-Jo ate soup. _____

_____

_____

_____

_____

_____

Carmen worked at the bookstore. _____

_____

_____

_____

_____

_____

He reached to hold Abigail's hand.

_____

_____

_____

_____

_____

_____

Nobody ever stood up to Bethany.

_____

_____

_____

_____

_____

Meena liked this hotel room.

_____

_____

_____

_____

_____

"Ladies and gentlemen, the first lady."

Minka had sat waiting for him all day.

Hannah had just gotten promoted.

Jody wasn't the only astronaut on the ship. _____

_____

_____

_____

_____

_____

_____

_____

_____

A World of Make-Believe

My first love were fantasy books. I remember, vividly, staying up until three or four in the morning, determined to finish the chapter (or, let's be honest, the book), ignoring that I would need to be up a few hours later for school. I have acclimated myself with the writers who have built mystical worlds, constructed whole cultures, and imagined new languages…and yet these fucks still can't come up with a mythical race that *isn't* white or write women who aren't fragile and codependent. I'm using present tense because I swear to all that is holy that every time I crack open a new fantasy novel by a white dude, it's the exact same shit, copy, paste.[*]

For all that, however, these crusty guys continue to be wildly successful. While one could argue that their success has been earned simply by their way with words, the savvier among us know differently. Sure, these men can spin a yarn, but that yarn also is chock-full of rape, euphemisms, and just outright weird descriptions of women's bodies. The author of *Game of Thrones*, George R. R. Martin, has said, ad nauseum, that the reason why he includes so much sexual violence in his novels is to be historically accurate.[**]

Yet *real history* shows us that during that the time frame that *Game of Thrones* is based on, in England, rape was still considered a crime—one that was punishable by death. A mere fifty years prior to the start of the War of the Roses, women were pardoned for tying up their rapist, cutting off his testicles, and stealing his horse because it was seen as justice for their rape. The punishment for the *Game of Thrones* rapists? Essentially nonexistent.

Sexual violence is only one of the hallmarks of male-written fantasy. Just as with most every other genre we've

* Although if I'm being totally honest, I truly cannot remember the last fantasy novel by a white man that I read. And look, I can appreciate that some of these guys were truly pioneers of the time and are the bedrock upon which much of fantasy is made. However, are you *really* trying to tell me that the streaming services and Best of Fantasy lists can't do better than remaking the work of an author who hasn't published anything new in the last ten years? *Yikes.*

** So historically accurate that he includes rape or attempted rape 214 times.

seen thus far, fantasy writers enjoy highlighting wholly odd sexual escapades and befuddling descriptions. Fantasy writers often get carried away with their purple prose, after all, when you're eight hundred pages deep in a world you carved from your imagination, it's only to be expected that you'd confuse breasts for mountains! Of course, only the women get this treatment because, as mentioned, they're fragile, delicate beings who must be protected by the Big Burly Men in their lives. Their only good use is for vague wisdom and child-rearing. A republican's dream.

But fantasy writers can teach us important lessons. Namely, that rules don't matter in the fantasy books we write. You want to describe a pair of tits as being as veined as blue cheese? Go for it. There's a certain freedom that comes from simply not giving a fuck, and it's a privilege that male writers have carried for too long. So let's test your lack of a fuck.

PROMPT: In the space below, make up a new mythical being. Describe this being first as a male and then as a female. Feel free to embrace the purple and go as far over the top as desired.

A Tale of Two Titties

The Slut's Scream

At long last we have reached the bread and butter of our lord and savior Stephen King.[*] In no uncertain terms, horror is overwhelmingly dominated by men. Be it the writer or the protagonist, reading horror is like walking into one of the Big Four consulting firms. Given how many of those who work there say they love *American Psycho*...well, I'm not wholly sure that's a coincidence. And if I'm being honest, reading horror as a woman is kind of like going on a blind first date: you never know if you'll be turned into a skin suit or if you'll make it out alive.[**]

Women in horror are lumped into two spectacular categories. They either find themselves as the first victim or the villain. Which, oddly, seems to speak to how most men view women, period. If she didn't bend over backwards to accommodate you in whichever way, she's the villain in your story. It's just with horror, she gets to be a monstrous villain with six mouths that all tell lies. In a handful of books, though more often in movies, a woman does survive, she is usually the Virgin, the purest or most naïve, and by the time she's driving away with flames in the rearview,

[*] My editors have informed me that, should I want a writing career beyond this book, I need to be careful in how often I mention St*phen K*ng. Stephen, if you're reading this, let's bury the axe over some martinis in Portland and discuss the merits of comparing breasts to punching bags or horrific gang rape scenes to bring a young girl into adulthood. No really, I'm waving the white flag, because I really would like to be a writer based on my merit and not penalized for calling out your many novels' blatant sexism.

[**] And I say this as someone who was naïve enough to fly down to a city to meet a boy who is my now husband. Is he wonderful? Yes. Was I sure I would be retrofitted into a lampshade? Also yes.

she's got a boatload of trauma to go along with that purity culture.

What can sometimes feel like the greatest horror of womanhood is that you are not believed, and horror movies and books are especially guilty of this. Often, that seems to be where the disconnect comes from for male writers with female readers. Men seem to be more concerned with the monster under their bed or the kooky clown who gives them a weird look, while women find fear with the catcaller who gets a little too close or the man who doesn't like being told no. Female characters beg to be believed about the monster while men are instantly given the benefit of the doubt.

Emerald Fennell's *Promising Young Woman* was a case study in the dichotomy of female and male horror and a lesson in that even the good guys can really fucking suck. When it comes to male horror, the bad guys are bad, plain and simple. They abuse kids or kick puppies, maybe the most morally grey they get is they have a Nagging Wife in the sheets but a murdered Whore in the streets. For women, it's the knowledge that even the "good guy" can be fucked up. And with all these horror novels being written by men, it's understandable that they would have a tenuous hold on what real horror is.

Writing horror from a male perspective means that, as a writer, you get to be more dramatic. Men aren't concerned about a man walking toward them at night on an empty sidewalk, and they don't worry about walking to their car in an empty parking lot. They don't carry mace or send tracking locations before they go on dates. Men are only scared when real shit goes down. As a result, the women in male-written horror books are fragile. Because men don't understand the day-to-day fear many women live in, they make the assumption that all women are fragile.

To keep up with the horror status quo, you must write women who fear everything and *do* everything that a woman in the real world simply wouldn't do. It's a complicated line to walk, and a hard mindset to put yourself into, which is why I've created the Bullshit Index. But more on that later.

PROMPT: For now, try your hand at writing a scene where your female character first encounters the monster that has killed all her friends.

A Tale of Two Titties

_____

_____

_____

_____

_____

_____

_____

_____

_____

_____

_____

_____

_____

_____

_____

_____

_____

_____

_____

_____

_____

_____

_____

_____

While it can be agnostic of any specific genre, the measurement known as the Bullshit Index is most often seen in horror. It was created to help aspiring writers like you compete with the male megawriters who seem to churn out a new novel overnight. While, as mentioned, all of these successful writers rely on stereotypes and tropes, as you are learning to do, they also write women who do the unbelievable. Just like in horror, female characters in *all* genres are put in situations that a real woman would never be found in. Men and women measure danger differently, but in your book, women can't be *more* fearless than men. Men need to have someone to save and a way to prove that they're better than everyone else.

Using the Bullshit Index will help you write women who are believable to men. These will be women who are scared of the dark, faint at the sight of blood, and wear heels to an amusement park crawling with prehistoric animals. The more unbelievable a situation, the higher it ranks on the Bullshit Index, and the more likely it is to be used in a book written by a man. More importantly than measurement, the Index will give the male protagonist ample opportunity to save the female character and to cement himself as a big heroic dude. That a woman would likely never get herself into that situation in the first place is not something you should ever think when constructing these scenarios. Women are feeble and stupid; that's why they need to stay at home.

The Bullshit Index is a great place to start with your first horror novel. Since so many women go through life with a fake phone number memorized to ward off the over aggressive barfly or wear fake wedding rings at work to prevent leering customers from being too forward, it can be hard to step back and put on the male gaze. You have to ask yourself what situation would your short-skirted female character put herself in that spits in the face of common sense? In these instances, we use the Bullshit Index.

The Bullshit Index

PROMPT: In the following spread, choose a number from the Bullshit Index and write a scene around the Muse of your choice.

10. Walking toward a mysterious noise
in a dark basement or alley

9. Having sex while
a killer is on the loose

8. Splitting up from a group of
friends in a sketchy situation

7. Going off the beaten track because a sketchy
dude at the gas station recommended it

6. While escaping, choosing to stop for the chainsaw
-wielding killer instead of plowing them over

5. Believing the blood-covered man who says he has nothing
to do with the murders, he was just in the wrong place

4. Hiding in the sketchy basement
with only one way out

3. Panicking and running off
without shoes on

2. Walking to a car, alone, at night,
in an empty parking lot

1. Going on a
blind date

BULLSHIT INDEX

A Tale of Two Titties

He Said, She Said

DESPITE THEIR MANY UNIQUE WAYS to terribly portray women, these mediums all have one struggle in common: dialogue. Maybe it's because they don't believe that women should speak, or even can speak, if there's not a man present. Maybe it's the thought process that if it isn't about handbags or dating, women simply never utter a word at all. Dialogue in every man-made medium is important; as every writer knows, dialogue is an integral part of every story. It's just that when it's from or between women, it matters a little bit less.

The Bechdel Test is a writer's worst enemy. First, it insists that a woman, and more than one be included in a work. And on top of that, they must discuss something other than men. Truly an eye-rolling phenomenon. The most successful of writers are those that dialogue from or among women can only stem from one of two invocations:

VAPID AND DEFERENTIAL—Also known as the type of language that occurs between our demurer muses like the Virgin, Librarian, or Secretary.

COMMANDING AND BITCHY—The strong language used by our Bosses, Femme Fatales, and on occasion, our Nagging Wives.

The subject matter, regardless of the tone must always center the male protagonist in some way, remember, no passing the Bechdel Test here. We don't care about the hopes, dreams, wants, or needs of any female character. Including reference to any of those things would imply that we care about her and that she matters to the story in a way that puts her on equal footing with the male protagonist, which simply can't happen.

An example that every aspiring writer should have pinned to their bulletin board as the ultimate passage on how to write women is the following, from James Wisher's *Darkness Rising*:

"Congratulations." She stepped back and looked at him. "You've grown so much."

"So have you," he said, eyeing her ample chest.

"Ugh! Why is it every boy, even my brother, notices those first? I swear they're nothing but a nuisance. Still, they make an excellent distraction when I fight men."

"I bet. What's for dinner?"

What does this add to the plot? Not a whole lot. But it does suggest that Wisher's female character has about two brain cells to rub together and has great tits, and as you ought to have learned by now, that's all that really matters so far as a woman being involved. The introduction of a female character with aspirations outside of those that the male protagonist has is a red flag that either the writer has no intention of being a best seller *or* that she's a handful of pages away from dying a long, painful death that the protagonist will reflect upon and use as revenge for years to come.

Dialogue is really just using everything you've learned thus far but applying it practically. This is also an ample opportunity to start to introduce dialect. *How* women speak can be more important than *what* they speak about. After all, there's a reason why the Valley Girl dialect has stuck around for so long—what better way to communicate to your viewers or readers that your female character is an idiot? Using abbreviated words or refusing to use contractions can show a character is low country or highbrow, and when used alongside with how she speaks to or about a male protagonist can communicate their relationship in the blink of an eye.

And as with most things, women being judged for how they speak is something that doesn't only live in fictitious works, it happens in real life, too. A 2017 study found that men are more likely than women to be speakers at academic conferences, not because women turned down the opportunity but simply because they were never extended the invitation. Not only are men the most prominent at these conferences, but they also talk the most.[*] And while in corporate America, men are the ones dominating important conversations on things like earning calls, it turns out that its women who make bolder and more accurate forecasts. It isn't just the corporate world either. Men talk more than women everywhere from the Supreme Court to classrooms.

* I would like to extend a formal fuck you to every man who ever told me I talked too much or too loudly.

And while men are obsessing over whether or not they can compliment a woman's outfit without being canceled,[*] women are having conversations on how to support each other if a man takes credit for their idea, is condescending, or speaks over them in a meeting. And perhaps for all these reasons, is it really a surprise that male writers think that women talk about nothing but men, if they ever talk at all?

This is the knowledge one must arm themselves with as they prepare to write the dialogue for their female characters. Men have been acting like women have nothing to contribute to the conversation for years, and none more so than male writers, who are happy to use a woman's mouth for a number of more unimaginable things than *conversation.*

* Hint: you can. I'm so tired of hearing men say, "Wah wah, I can't compliment women on anything anymore!" Yes, you can, just don't objectify them? There's literally no reason you can't just say, verbatim, "Mia, I really like your haircut." I am *begging* men to realize that it isn't that you can't compliment women, it's that you can't objectify us or stare at our tits all the time and think we're going to be OK with that.

INSTRUCTIONS: Embrace what you've learned so far and, in the space below, construct a scene between Dan and his assistant Marina where they're discussing what's on Dan's calendar.

A Tale of Two Titties

Breast Exam

It is now time to test your knowledge. You have spent much of this workbook learning about exciting fruits to compare breasts to* and familiarizing yourself with the Muses. Hopefully by now you'll have learned that male writers always know best, after all, that's why they're continuously at the top of the bestsellers lists! Passing this test is the key to success and will prove to yourself and other writers that you deserve to write a novel. The importance of this test cannot be stressed enough; men are raised to know that they are better than women if for no other reason than the penis they wield. They are told their voices are the ones that deserve to be heard, their work is coddled, and their successes are heralded. And while some writers may complain** that it's hard to be an older, white man in today's world, the truth of the matter is that it's about time that they had some competition.

And really, what better way to stick it to them than to beat them at their own game? The Breast Exam on the next page will see how far you've come and test how ready you are to run with the Pattersons, Grishams, Murakamis, and Kings of the world. So grab your pencil, and let's begin.

* Yuzu could be a fun one to try next!

** One would think that it's common sense that white men have been dominating the book world for ages, but James Patterson thinks otherwise. In a 2022 article, he said that he worries that it's hard for white men to get writing jobs, and that it's "just another form of racism." According to him, "It's even harder for older writers. You don't meet many fifty-two-year-old white males."

BREAST EXAM

1. **When describing a pair of breasts, one might best use the imagery of:**

   Ⓐ Fists

   Ⓑ Apples

   Ⓒ Punching bags

   Ⓓ All of the above

2. **When describing a woman, you should first take into account:**

   Ⓐ Her appearance

   Ⓑ Her actions

3. **When writing a thriller, if a woman runs away screaming, she will most likely be later discovered brutally killed.**

   Ⓐ True

   Ⓑ False

4. **If a female character asks her husband to feed the children dinner, she is:**

   Ⓐ A Matron

   Ⓑ A Nagging Wife

   Ⓒ A Whore

   Ⓓ None of the above

5. **Should a writer's novel be optioned for a movie, female characters should be:**

   Ⓐ Dressed in revealing clothes regardless of plot

   Ⓑ Given speaking parts as meaty as their male counterparts

   Ⓒ Treated with respect

6. The ability for a man to make his female partner orgasm every time is called:

Ⓐ The Cock Conundrum

Ⓑ The Casanova Mandate

Ⓒ The Magic Dick Directive

7. Barbara has just discovered a map to the Lost City of Chae in the library. How should she tell the lead explorer, Todd, what she found? Choose the line of dialogue that best fits:

Ⓐ "I found it, Todd! Turns out you had us looking in the wrong place!"

Ⓑ "Stay here and see if you can discover anything else, Todd. I'll go get the rest of the group ready."

Ⓒ "I can't believe you missed it, Todd. The map was here the whole time!"

Ⓓ "Oh Todd, you were right, the map *was* in the library! Thank goodness you were here to point me in the right direction. You know how confused I get."

8. When describing female anatomy, it is imperative that you:

Ⓐ Compare it to a fruit, flower, or other item in nature so as to give the reader something to envision

Ⓑ Are as accurate as possible, using the actual scientific terms

Ⓒ Don't describe it at all

9. The method used to measure how realistic an event is to happen to a woman in horror is called:

Ⓐ The Gut Check for Girls

Ⓑ The Bullshit Index

Ⓒ The Horrometer

Ⓓ The Slut's Scream

10. In fiction, the role of a woman is to:

Ⓐ Uplift the man

Ⓑ Manifest her own destiny

Ⓒ Follow in her family's footsteps

11. Romance is a respectable genre of fiction for any aspiring writer:

Ⓐ True

Ⓑ False

12. If you need inspiration for how to describe breasts, you should:

Ⓐ Ask a woman in your life

Ⓑ Move on. If you're struggling, you shouldn't describe them at all

Ⓒ Go to the grocer for inspiration

Ⓓ Open a textbook

13. If questioned on how you're writing women, you should always say:

Ⓐ Nothing, you should never engage

Ⓑ That it was an accident and you'll change it

Ⓒ It's just the way your character thinks

14. A woman's profession can be used to best:

Ⓐ Figure out how to objectify her

Ⓑ Help the male protagonist to relate to her

15. It is OK to use words inaccurately as long as they sound good and fit the vibe of your scene.

Ⓐ True

Ⓑ False

16. If the male protagonist needs an encouraging pep talk, which Muse should he turn to?

Ⓐ The Femme Fatale

Ⓑ The Virgin

Ⓒ The Matron

17. Louise has been helping Larry on a science experiment to prove that pigs fly for the last five years. While Larry is on holiday, Louise discovers that some pigs are born with an air bladder, allowing them to take flight. Who should get credit for this discovery?

Ⓐ Larry, it's his experiment after all

Ⓑ Louise, because she found the air bladder

18. After what felt like hours of waiting, Tana, Mark's number one assassin, finally appeared. She was dressed in a skintight catsuit, which _____. Fill in the blank.

Ⓐ Allowed her to have complete mobility

Ⓑ Emphasized her full breasts, the partially unzipped top showcasing them like mountain peaks

Ⓒ Meant she could creep through their target location totally undetected

19. If the female character's anatomy doesn't obey the laws of gravity, you are most likely writing:

Ⓐ Fantasy

Ⓑ Science Fiction

Ⓒ Horror

20. The key to writing women is to:

Ⓐ Write them as you would a man

Ⓑ Base them on real women you know

Ⓒ Reduce them to simple stereotypes for the everyday person to understand

The Balance of Fame and Fortune

17

SO LONG AS YOU FOLLOW the directives of this workbook, your fame will be right around the corner, and with that fame comes a certain set of knowledge that typically must be learned on the fly. However, what sort of teacher am I if I don't give you the tools to succeed even after you've left the nest? Male authors act as if they're entitled to their successes, that they have *always* deserved to be published and recognized and it was just a matter of time. There is an air of it that wafts from longstanding successful men who know that they've been a part of the bestseller list for so long they'll never fail. It's why so many of them are able to make such blasé statements about the fate of the world as it affects them, forgetting that their experience is not the same as everyone else's.

And of course, they like to give back to fellow writers. Just, you know, not to anyone who doesn't look like them.

These men are above mistakes. A spelling error? Intentional. Misogyny entwined with every plot they've ever crafted? A part of their character's arc, even if it's a different character in every novel. This sense of being untouchable and entitled is one they were born with, but it's one you must learn if you wish to have an iota of the success for yourself. As readers, we wonder if these men have editors, but the more realistic answer is that they do and they just don't care.

In practice, this takes many forms, and just as you must find which genre best fits you, so must you find how best to practice your entitlement. For some writers, this looks like acting as if your writing is a gift to the world. If a fan questions how long it's taking you to write, block them on social media or berate them publicly as you wax poetic about your "process." Other famous authors like to take their stories and essentially rewrite them years after they were published in an effort to stay relevant and to pretend to be progressive.* Whatever your

* And to She Who Must Not Be Named, trans women are women. Maybe if you'd spent more time focused on being an ally and a good person and less on being an Extremely Online TERF, you wouldn't have been compared to Putin.

method, should you ever be questioned about it, be sure to dig in your heels and insist that you know best because, after all, you're famous and your fans are not.

Of course, many would argue that the ideal life of a writer is one where you can live off your work and then disappear into a cottage by the sea. A warm fireplace, cozy socks, a pet to keep you company, and ample land for you to walk out your ideas. Unfortunately, that is simply not a feasible reality for most writers. In today's world, many writers are expected to market themselves and their book to a certain degree. The spate of social media platforms out in the world certainly help, which is a blessing considering that even *book marketing* prioritizes male writers over female.

Male writers receive 56 percent of review coverage, and when women *are* reviewed, the interviews and reviews revolve around her personal life and not the work itself.[*] Female writers are often viewed as hobbyists who write about women's issues[**] or romance while their male counterparts are given legitimacy even before the quality of their work is judged. That male writers are often given more and better tools to succeed in the first place is not a fact that is lost on me.

[*] Which, all things considered, isn't wholly surprising given that there's a *plethora* of interviews with female models, celebrities, and CEOs that focus on the color of her eyes and curve of her lips. It can sometimes feel like the work that women do isn't nearly as important as how they look while doing it.

[**] That "women's literature" is an entire subgenre of fiction is insulting, and a huge part of the problem itself. The term implies that only women will read those books, with the thought process being that the books center around family or domestic life. Of course, there is no "men's literature" section...that's just a bookstore.

This workbook has given you some of those tools to get that kick start that most men are born with, and some of the secrets of why those tools are so successful in the first place. What you do with that success, ultimately, is up to you. History has shown us, though, that it's the men who go on to pocket that cold, hard cash. And movies are just as guilty as books. In 2021, 85 percent of films had more male than female characters, with women making up less than one third of sole protagonists in film.

Sure, we can pull ourselves up by our bootstraps, but it isn't so much nicer to get a leg up?

Using the bag of tricks found in this workbook, we will be able to infiltrate their ranks and overcome them, transforming the system from the inside out while also making sure that we can benefit too.

The Manifesto

Since I can't exactly make you swear a blood oath to write like a man,[*] I've decided to bequeath you the next best thing: a manifesto. I'm not asking for much, just that you sign the dotted line, commit to writing your breast so long as you walk this Earth, and tattoo it on your arm. Or pin it up next to your desk. I'm not picky. This is hardly a big ask. After all, men do it every day! The Manifesto is your commitment to the art of describing breasts like fruit and the science of, well, making up your own science. In doing so, I ask that you pass down the secrets within these pages to others like you, others who are not men and aspire to see their words splashed across reviews, atop bestsellers lists, and optioned into film.

There's a host of male writers who have no qualms over writing under a female pen name in order to speak to a female audience,[**] so really, they shouldn't be too bothered by women writing like them!

On the following page, fill in your name as a commitment to the cause. At the bottom, sign your name to promise to follow in the footsteps of the misogynists before you.

[*] For legal reasons, my editor would like me to clarify that this is a joke and doing so is at your own risk. Additionally, women signing their names in blood hasn't historically worked out for them. See also: the Salem Witch Trials.

[**] Dean Koontz has used the names Deanna Dwyer and Leigh Nichols, the bestselling Spanish author Carmen Mola turned out to be three men writing under a pseudonym, and even Carolyn Keene, the author behind the beloved Nancy Drew books, isn't a real person but rather a host of authors (including men).

I, _____, hereafter referred to as THE WRITER, do so promise that my word is my bond, and in signing this document, I promise to live my authorly life based on the Manifesto below.

We acknowledge that men have had a chokehold on the world of literature for far too long. We are prepared to have the audacity of subpar bestsellers and prepare to join them in the trenches of misogyny. They've gone low, so we will go lower, subterranean, even, in pursuit of fruity breasts and instant orgasms. We will defend the noble pursuit of author-hood with leering descriptions of women in the spirit of the time-honored tradition of Men Know Best. We do this with bitterness in our hearts and spite in our veins, so that our names may be at the top of the bestsellers list.

With this signature, I vow to write my breast until such time as female writers are given the respect they deserve.

Signature: _____

Date: _____

With these words you are now part of the Write Your Breast community, the one you never knew you needed. Whenever you're struck dumb with that weaselly bastard called writer's block, you need only remember your forefathers and the work they so dutifully created. May you be inspired by the drivel they wrote, and got *published*, and know that you, too, can join their ranks. As one of us, you have a whole gang of bosom buddies at your side, ready to come to your aid, one titty at a time.

18

The Heart of the Matter

WRITING THIS BOOK WAS AN adventure in misogyny. When I told men I met what *A Tale of Two Titties* was about, many of them laughed at me. The excuses for the male writers that they know and love were endless—from reasoning that that's how things were to the character being an asshole (even if it was a new character every time) to the age-old excuse that it wasn't that big of a deal. And while it's true that there's something comical about reading breasts described as cantaloupes or ships, liberties that some male authors feel they can take with a woman's body is absurd. The reality is that writing women like they're nothing more than tits on legs that exist for the sole pleasure of men has real world implications.

Teaching books by almost exclusively male authors to students shows them that men's voices deserve to be heard over women and that it's acceptable, even today, to talk about women like objects. The point is driven home when that language is used in day-to-day life, be it how men speak to women or about them. Normalizing it further solidifies it, meaning women get objectified by men everywhere, whether it's on dating apps or by politicians. And because it's such a part of our culture, it's a hard thing to simply stop doing. When men are called out on the sexism they're expressing, they take it as a character attack. "Ugh, I can't even compliment a woman," they huff, as if all there are to a woman are her breasts and ass.

Books are a key part of who we are, and those we read can greatly affect not only how we view the world but how we speak. It's foolish to think that the centuries-old trend of writing women like we don't deserve pleasure or respect hasn't seeped into our daily lives, and simply ignoring that it has doesn't get us anywhere. The purpose of this book isn't to remove books by men from circulation. It's about showing just how outrageous it is to write women without any semblance of autonomy. While I think it would be great if John Grisham and Stephen King acknowledged the not-so-subtle misogyny and fatphobia in their books, and would even settle for them no longer doing it, the truth of the matter is that isn't going to happen.

Writers include food-centric descriptions of breasts, instantaneous orgasms, and magical vaginas with a wink and a nod. These are men who can spend months, if not years, researching everything from the way that blood splatters to how the Ottoman Empire fell, but when it comes to women, for some reason it's easier to simply pretend. We are the *here there be dragons* on a map, worth imagining but not encountering and better kept to the fantastical. That women are real creates more problems than not, and instead of acknowledging the poor job they've done writing women, male authors would prefer to just keep doing what they've always done.

Similarly, men will continue to objectify women because, as a society, we have deemed that it's an acceptable thing to do. With these men topping bestsellers lists on a consistent basis, it's frustrating to see that still, misogyny sells. Authors are still digging their heels in in favor of "artistic integrity" or "accuracy" or some other bullshit that they think can forgive them of their behavior. Male politicians are actively working on removing women's rights across the country, our health system continuously ignores the voices of Black and female patients, and companies continue to punish women for choosing to have families.

It's important to have these conversations with friends and loved ones, because while dismantling the patriarchy won't happen overnight, it can be taken down brick by brick. Just because these writers objectify their female characters doesn't mean they're inherently bad people; it just means that they're part of a system that's done nothing but work for them their entire life. But it's noticing that system that is imperative. Using humor as a tool to help people notice this kind of casual misogyny, instead of an accusatory "why didn't you notice!?" voice, was one of the core goals of *A Tale of Two Titties*. If the only thing a reader takes away from this book is simply noticing, the workbook will have succeeded.

Complacency is how this narrative continues, which means more stories where women are nothing but tits and can never be the hero of their own story. While this workbook is meant, in part, to serve as an opportunity to have a joke at the expense of the men who have been using women as the butt of theirs, it's also to point out just how outrageous and commonplace their misogyny is. And fuck it, worst case scenario, we learn their ways, call them out on their bullshit, and start knocking them off the pedestals they've put themselves on.

But mostly, I hope that more women and nonbinary folks take this as an opportunity to realize that their voices deserve and need to be heard. The quotes in this workbook are from real men, the stories of men taking credit are true, and I'd bet a boatload of money that none of them feel guilty about it. White men have been dominating the literary canon for far too long, getting the brunt of marketing publicity, film options, and acknowledgement for work that really isn't up to par. If nothing else, use this workbook as ammunition to take a chance on yourself. Men have been assuming that whatever they touch is magnificent since they were born, so let yourself believe that you can actually write work that is worthy of being written.

If all else fails, pick a masculine-sounding pen name and just write your breast.

Acknowledgments

When I first began writing, I never would've imagined that my first book would be nonfiction. That it is largely fueled by spite, however, does make a lot of sense. I began the Men Write Women Twitter account several years ago in an effort to have real conversations around the impact that misogyny in fiction has on our real lives. I didn't want to simply post examples; I wanted to call out *why* it was wrong, to have conversations around the ripple effect, and maybe even change a few minds. The community that has since grown from a few spicy tweets has been truly surreal.

But bridging the gap between Twitter and book couldn't have been possible without my agents, Maggie Cooper and Justin Brouckaert—I thank my lucky stars every day that I didn't mark that email as spam. Thank you for being my coaches and confidants throughout this whole process. But most of all, thank you for believing in me. My amazing editor,

Kate Roddy, and the entire team over at Sourcebooks, who made sure that this book was coherent. I am so grateful for each and every one of you. Kate, thank you for thinking I'm funny, for finding smarts in my snark, and for catching every word I missed in the mad keyboard mash of writing.

To the men I quote, it's nothing personal. Some of you are talented storytellers, but perhaps it's time you realized your work would be better without the heavy dollop of misogyny you seem to think you need.

This book never would've come to fruition without the cheerleading and belief of my friends and family, and so it cannot go into the world without giving thanks to them.

To my parents, while I can't say that, as a kid, I loved the red pen that marked my every essay, I am grateful for how you both made me a better writer. I hope you don't feel the need to break it out for this. I am so grateful to have grown up in a home where I had two creative role models to look up to. To my siblings, Ginny and George, thank you, always, for thinking this is as fucking cool as I do.

To Rachel, my partner in wine and bad scary movies, I am so lucky to have a best friend who believes in me as much as you do. I love you even though you have shit taste in wine. The next bottle of red is on me. To Caitlin, I have never been more grateful for nosebleed concert tickets—thanks for always picking up the phone.

And finally, to Ryan. Thank you for providing wine and stacks of books for inspiration and "just because," for staving off fears of failure with an unending supply of sour gummy worms and dark chocolate, and for re-reading endless passages to make sure they're funny and not unhinged. There aren't enough words to express how grateful I am for you and how much I love you. I am so glad to have found a partner who loves storytelling, in all its forms, just as much as I do.

References

"9 Scientists Who Didn't Get the Credit They Deserved." Oxford Royale Academy. Accessed July 24, 2022. https://www.oxford-royale.com/articles/9-scientists -didnt-get-credit-deserved/.

"About the Author." David Foster Wallace Books. Accessed July 25, 2022. http://www .davidfosterwallacebooks.com/about.html.

Alli. "Women Who Had Their Work Stolen from Them by Men." History Collection. Accessed July 24, 2022. https://historycollection.com/women-who-had-their -work-stolen-from-them-by-men/2/.

Auerbach, Jonathan. *Male Call: Becoming Jack London.* Durham: Duke University Press, 1996.

Baxter, Sarah. "James Patterson: White Male Writers Are Victims of 'Racism'." *Sunday Times,* Sunday 12, 2022. https://www.thetimes.co.uk/article/james-patterson -white-male-writers-are-victims-of-racism-bzqj50fj3.

"Bechdel Test Movie List." Bechdel Test. Accessed July 30, 2022. https://bechdeltest.com/.

Beil, Laura. "A Surgeon So Bad It Was Criminal." ProPublica, October 2, 2018. https://www.propublica.org/article/dr-death-christopher-duntsch-a-surgeon -so-bad-it-was-criminal.

Berman, Marc. "Serena Acted Like a Sore Loser." *New York Post*, September 9, 2018. https://nypost.com/2018/09/08/serena-acted-like-a-sore-loser/.

Berman, Marc. "Novak Djuokovic's Excessive Punishment is Terrible for US Open."

New York Post, September 6, 2020. https://nypost.com/2020/09/06/novak-djokovics -disqualification-is-terrible-for-the-us-open/.

Maranz, Felice, and Rebecca Greenfield. "Men Get the First, Last and Every Other Word on Earnings Calls." Bloomberg News, September 13, 2018. https://www.bloomberg.com/news/articles/2018-09-13/men-get-the-first-last-and -every-other-word-on-earnings-calls.

Bolter, Kylie. "Final Girl Trope: The Girl Boss-ification of Horror Movies Not as Feminist as Male Directors Think It Is." Hollywood Insider, October 30, 2021. https://www.hollywoodinsider.com/final-girl-trope/.

Broster, Alice. "What is the Orgasm Gap?" *Forbes*, July 21, 2020. https://www.forbes .com/sites/alicebroster/2020/07/31/what-is-the-orgasm-gap/.

Cowper-Cowles, Minna. "Women Political Leaders: The Impact of Gender on Democracy." Westminster Foundation for Democracy, March 25, 2021. https://www.wfd.org /what-we-do/resources/women-political-leaders-impact-gender-democracy.

"Did Joss Whedon Nearly Have a Bleak Rape Plot on Firefly?" Legends Revealed, August 24, 2016. https://legendsrevealed.com/entertainment/2016/08/24/did-joss -whedon-nearly-have-a-bleak-rape-plot-on-firefly/.

Encyclopaedia Britannica Online, s.v. "Adam and Eve." Accessed June 11, 2022. https://www.britannica.com/biography/Adam-and-Eve-biblical-literary-figures.

Faure, Valentine, and Thomas Chatterton Williams. "Emily Ratajkowski: Peut-on être féministe et n'exister que par son corps?" *Marie Claire* (French edition). Accessed August 5, 2022. https://www.marieclaire.fr/emily-ratajkowski-peut-on -etre-feministe-et-n-exister-que-par-son-corps,1276946.asp.

Fellizar, Kristine. "Weaponized Incompetence, the Common Form of Gaslighting That's Trending on TikTok." Bustle, October 20, 2021. https://www.bustle.com /wellness/weaponized-incompetence-manipulation-tactic.

Flood, Alison. "Male and Female Writers' Media Coverage Reveals 'Marked Bias'."

Guardian, March 18, 2019. https://www.theguardian.com/books/2019/mar/18 /male-and-female-writers-media-coverage-reveals-marked-bias.

George-Parkin, Hilary. "The Power of Dressing—How Female Politicians Use Clothes to Send a Message." The Zoe Report, January 26, 2021. https://www.thezoereport .com/culture/how-female-politicians-use-fashion-to-send-a-message.

Gerstein, Josh, and Alexander Ward. "Supreme Court Has Voted to Overturn Abortion Rights, Draft Opinion Shows." *Politico*, April 2, 2022. https://www.politico.com /news/2022/05/02/supreme-court-abortion-draft-opinion-00029473

Gharib, Malaka. "Real Orgasms and Transcendent Pleasure: How Women Are Reigniting Desire." NPR, February 14, 20200. https://www.npr.org/sections /health-shots/2020/02/14/803725591/real-orgasms-and-transcendent-pleasure -how-women-are-reigniting-desire.

Grady, Constance. "Roman Polanski is Now Facing a Fifth Accusation of Sexual Assault Against a Child." Vox, October 23, 2017. https://www.vox.com/culture /2017/8/17/16156902/roman-polanski-child-rape-charges-explained-samantha -geimer-robin-m.

Grady, Constance. "Black Authors Are on All the Bestseller Lists Right Now. But Publishing Doesn't Pay Them Enough." Vox, June 17, 2020. https:// www.vox.com/culture/2020/6/17/21285316/publishing-paid-me-diversity -black-authors-systemic-bias.

Harris, Carissa. "800 Years of Rape Culture." Aeon, May 24, 2021. https://aeon.co /essays/the-hypocrisies-of-rape-culture-have-medieval-roots.

Hoyle, Alexander Miserlis, Lawrence Wolf-Sonkin, Hanna Wallach, Isabelle Augenstein, and Ryan Cotterell. "Unsupervised Discovery of Gendered Language through Latent-Variable Modeling." *Proceedings of the 57th Annual Meeting of the Association for Computational Linguistics* (July 2019): 1706–1716. https://doi.org/10.18653/v1 /p19-1167.

Izhac, Suad. "The Gender Bias in Book Marketing." The Boar, April 9, 2019. https://theboar.org/2019/04/gender-bias-book-marketing/.

Johnson, Charles. "How H.G. Wells Predicted the 20th Century." *New York Time*, November 19, 2021. https://www.nytimes.com/2021/11/19/books/review/the-young-hg-wells-claire-tomalin.html.

King, Hope. "The Easy Life of 'Mediocre' Men." Axios, June 18, 2021. https://www.axios.com/2021/06/18/mediocre-men-fail-up-women-workplace.

King, Rachel. "The Romance Novel Sales Boom Continues." *Fortune,* August 21, 2021. https://fortune.com/2021/08/21/rom-com-pandemic-book-sales-romance-bookstore-day/.

Lesses, Rebecca. "Lilith." In *Shalvi/Hyman Encyclopedia of Jewish Women*. Jewish Women's Archive. Accessed June 11, 2022. https://jwa.org/encyclopedia/article/lilith.

Levin, Bess. "GOP Lawmaker Likens Human Women to Sea Turtles to Explain Why They Don't Deserve Rights." *Vanity Fair*, May 11, 2022. https://www.vanityfair.com/news/2022/05/steve-daines-sea-turtle-eggs-abortion.

Lu, Jennifer. "How a Parasitic Fungus Turns Ants into 'Zombies'." *National Geographic*, April 18, 2019. https://www.nationalgeographic.com/animals/article/cordyceps-zombie-fungus-takes-over-ants.

Mariani, Gael. "Henrietta Leavitt—Celebrating the Forgotten Astronomer." aavso. Accessed July 24, 2022. https://www.aavso.org/henrietta-leavitt-%E2%80%93-celebrating-forgotten-astronomer.

Meg (@menwtirewomen). "fuck mary shelley amirite??" Twitter, November 20, 2021, 7:37 p.m. https://twitter.com/menwritewomen/status/1462218536315666435.

Miller, Brittany. "George R. R. Martin: 'Game of Thrones' Isn't 'Misogynistic'— It's Just Real Life." *New York Post*, July 25, 2022. https://nypost.com/2022/07/25/george-r-r-martin-game-of-thrones-isnt-anti-woman/.

"Missing Persons Statistics 2022." Black and Missing Foundation. Accessed July 16, 2022, from https://blackandmissinginc.com/statistics/.

Nittrouer, Christine L., Michelle R. Behl, Leslie Ashburn-Nardo, Rachel C. E. Trump-Steele, David M. Lane, and Virginia Valian. "Gender Disparities in Colloquium Speakers at Top Universities." *Proceedings of the National Academy of Sciences* 115, no. 1 (December 18, 2017): 104–108, https://doi.org/10.1073/pnas.1708414115.

North, Anna. "Historically, Men Translated the Odyssey. Here's What Happened When a Woman Took the Job." Vox, November 20, 2017. https://www.vox.com/identities/2017/11/20/16651634/odyssey-emily-wilson-translation-first-woman-english.

Ogren, Thomas Leo. "Botanical Sexism Cultivates Home-Grown Allergies." *Scientific American* (blog), April 29, 2015. https://blogs.scientificamerican.com/guest-blog/botanical-sexism-cultivates-home-grown-allergies/.

Plevkova, Jana, Mariana Brozmanova, Jana Harsanyiova, Miroslav Sterusky, Jan Honetschlager, and Tomas Buday. "Various Aspects of Sex and Gender Bias in Biomedical Research." *Physiological Research* 69 (December 2020): S367–S378, https://doi.org/10.33549%2Fphysiolres.934593.

Rowland, Katherine. "I Spent Five Years Talking to Women Across the U.S. about Pleasure and Desire. Here's What I Learned about Inequality in the Bedroom." *Time*, January 31, 2020. https://time.com/5775442/sexual-relationships-inequality/.

Ryzik, Melena, Cara Buckley, and Jodi Kanto. "Louis C. K. Is Accused by 5 Women of Sexual Misconduct." *New York Times*, November 8, 2017. https://www.nytimes.com/2017/11/09/arts/television/louis-ck-sexual-misconduct.html.

Saperstein, Pat. "Only 7% of Movies in 2021 Featured More Women than Men, Study Finds." *Variety*, March 15, 2022. https://variety.com/2022/film/news/womens-roles-2021-films-men-outnumber-lauzen-study-1235204838/.

Schumann, Megan. "The Orgasm Gap Continues With Women Expecting Less During Intimacy." Rutgers University (blog), April 5, 2022. https://www.rutgers.edu/news/orgasm-gap-continues-women-expecting-less-during-intimacy.

Smith, Yvette. "Katherine Johnson: The Girl Who Loved to Count." NASA (blog). Updated March 2, 2020. https://www.nasa.gov/feature/katherine-johnson-the-girl-who-loved-to-count/.

Spiegel, Josh. "'Wonder Woman' Is a Milestone, But It Shouldn't Be." *Hollywood Reporter*, June 4, 2017. https://www.hollywoodreporter.com/movies/movie-news/wonder-woman-is-a-milestone-but-shouldnt-be-1010023/.

"Supreme Court Nominee Brett Kavanaugh Sexual Assault Hearing, Judge Kavanaugh Testimony." C-Span, September 27, 2018. Video, 3:00:00. https://www.c-span.org/video/?451895-2%2Fsupreme-court-nominee-brett-kavanaugh-sexual-assault-hearing-judge-kavanaugh-testimony.

Tafkar. "Rape in ASOIAF vs. Game of Thrones: A Statistical Analysis." Tafkar (blog), May 24, 2015. https://tafkarfanfic.tumblr.com/post/119770640640/rape-in-asoiaf-vs-game-of-thrones-a-statistical.

"The Golden Age of Comics." History Detectives Special Investigations. PBS. Accessed July 30, 2022. https://www.pbs.org/opb/historydetectives/feature/the-golden-age-of-comics/.

Thomas, Dexter. "Oscar-nominated 'Hidden Figures' Was Whitewashed—But It Didn't Have to Be." Vice, January 25, 2017. https://www.vice.com/en/article/d3xmja/oscar-nominated-hidden-figures-was-whitewashed-but-it-didnt-have-to-be.

"Timeline of Attacks on Abortion: 2009–2021." Planned Parenthood. Accessed June 11, 2022. https://www.plannedparenthoodaction.org/issues/abortion/abortion-central-history-reproductive-health-care-america/timeline-attacks-abortion.

Toomey, Emily. "Ten Things We've Learned About Linons Since Disney's Original 'The Lion King'." *Smithsonian*, July 19, 2019. https://www.smithsonianmag.com/science-nature/ten-things-weve-learned-about-lions-disneys-original-lion-king-180972689/.

"Tubal Ligation." Johns Hopkins Medicine (blog). Accessed June 11, 2022. https://www.hopkinsmedicine.org/health/treatment-tests-and-therapies/tubal-ligation.

Tucker, Ian. "The Five: Unsung Female Scientists." *Guardian*, June 16, 2019. https://www.theguardian.com/science/2019/jun/16/the-five-unsung-female-scientists-overlook-credit-stolen-jean-purdy.

Walsh, Savannah. "Louis C. K. Wins a Grammy for His Comedy Album about Cancellation." *Vanity Fair*, April 4, 2022. https://www.vanityfair.com/hollywood/2022/04/louis-ck-wins-a-grammy-for-his-comedy-album-about-cancellation.

Wells, Veronica. "On the Problematic and Unnecessary White Saviors in Hidden Figures." MadameNoire, January 21, 2017. https://madamenoire.com/784290/on-the-problematic-and-unnecessary-white-saviors-in-hidden-figures/.

Wikipedia, s.v. "List of Awards and Nominations Received by Roman Polanski." Accessed June 8, 2022. https://en.wikipedia.org/wiki/List_of_awards_and_nominations_received_by_Roman_Polanski.

Wikipedia, s.v. "Invisible Man." Accessed July 25, 2022. https://en.wikipedia.org/wiki/Invisible_Man.